a Life of
SIGNIFICANCE

CAMMY WALTERS

a Life of SIGNIFICANCE

TATE PUBLISHING
AND ENTERPRISES, LLC

A Life of Significance
Copyright © 2014 by Cammy Walters. All rights reserved.

No part of this publication may be reproduced, stored in a retrieval system or transmitted in any way by any means, electronic, mechanical, photocopy, recording or otherwise without the prior permission of the author except as provided by USA copyright law.

This book is designed to provide accurate and authoritative information with regard to the subject matter covered. This information is given with the understanding that neither the author nor Tate Publishing, LLC is engaged in rendering legal, professional advice. Since the details of your situation are fact dependent, you should additionally seek the services of a competent professional.

The opinions expressed by the author are not necessarily those of Tate Publishing, LLC.

Published by Tate Publishing & Enterprises, LLC
127 E. Trade Center Terrace | Mustang, Oklahoma 73064 USA
1.888.361.9473 | www.tatepublishing.com

Tate Publishing is committed to excellence in the publishing industry. The company reflects the philosophy established by the founders, based on Psalm 68:11,
"The Lord gave the word and great was the company of those who published it."

Book design copyright © 2014 by Tate Publishing, LLC. All rights reserved.
Cover design by Junriel Boquecosa
Interior design by Jimmy Sevilleno

Published in the United States of America
ISBN: 978-1-63306-963-3
1. Religion / Christian Education / General
2. Religion / Christian Life / Spiritual Growth
14.08.14

I WOULD LIKE to dedicate this book first to anyone who feels that their life doesn't mean anything and isn't worth much. Through this book, you will see that your life is a significant life and without you we would miss everything that you have to offer us and your insight that you have to share with each of us including the Golden God Nuggets that God deposited into your life.

The second group that I would like to dedicate this book to is to all of my children; Jamie, Jennifer, Johnathan, Sasha, Donald, John, and Marcus. Without each of you, I would not have had the pleasure of having you as a part of my life, or learning the many lessons that you have brought into my life through the years, nor would I have learned about the many facets of God through your lives being connected to mine. Each of you has made me a better person, by God allowing me to be your Mom on this Earth.

Last, but never least I want to dedicate this book to my husband Don. You have taught me the true meaning of life and love, and I am truly grateful to God for having brought you into my life, you are the best part of me. You have truly been an inspiration to me, and I love and appreciate you so much. I am truly a blessed woman.

Acknowledgements

First I want to thank God for allowing me the awesome privilege to write a timely book to help so many hurting and wounded people throughout the world. I also want to thank my good friend and editor; Nancy Shoop that spent tireless hours encouraging me and editing this book as I wrote it.

Not that there is an order to the importance that you played in your contribution that each of you have made in the writing of this book, but I did want to thank each and every one of you that shared your life changing stories to bring this book to fruition. Without your willingness to share your lives none of this would have been possible. I am sending a huge thank you to Joann, Ferris, Karen, Tommy, Keagan, Shelly, Rickey, John, Miss Joy, Lisa (Sorry I left your name out of the book in the first edition),Bella, Rachel, Jeanie and Amy for all of the Golden God nuggets that you have shared.

I want a special thank you to go to my dear friends Dan and Becky for graciously providing my author photographs and introducing me to Joann for this book. Each of you are blessings to Don and me, and so near and dear to my heart, never would I have guessed that the Lord would have provided me with such blessings.

Contents

Introduction 11
Section I: Planned Arrivals. 15
   1: The Conception Of Life. 17
   2: Marcus The Sole Survivor 21
   3: Keagan's Prophetic Entrance 27
   #1 Points To Ponder. 37
Section II: Unexpected Blessings 41
   4: Jesus – Prophesied About But Still Unexpected . . . 43
   5: John And His Halo!. 47
   6: Sasha Our Minister Of Mercy. 53
   7: Johnathan's Touch – Part One 59
   #2 Points To Ponder. 65
Section III: Adoption Into A New Life 69
   8: Johnathan's Touch – Part Two
   Birth Mother Prays To An Unknown God 71
   9: Donald The Destined Son 77
   10: Tori's Arrival 87
   #3 Points To Ponder. 95

Section IV: An Aborted Life 99
   11: Shawna's Soul Tie 101
   12: John Is My Brother 105
   13: Amy's Fragments 109
   #4 Points To Ponder. 115

Section V: Miscarriage Of Expectation 119
   14: Tobi's Birth Meant Death 121
   15: The Resurrection Life Of Ike. 131
   #5 Points To Ponder. 139

Section VI: Stolen Lives And The Blessings
That They Leave Behind. 143
   16: Misty Lynn's Legacy 145
   17: Bella's Smile. 155
   18: Jeanie's Journey 161
   #6 Points To Ponder. 167

Section VII: Golden God Nuggets Lessons
Gleaned And Hope Restored 169
   19: Daughter Of Joy. 171
   20: Rachel's Story. 177
   21: Gathering The Fragments 187
   Final Points To Ponder 193

About The Author 197

Suggested Reading List Of Topics Presented
Within This Book. 203

Book Review. 207

Introduction

THREE STRIKES UPON the music stand in front of the Conductor signals the attention of the entire orchestra. He raises his hands, and begins the concert performance titled "All about You".

Every person has a specific plan and purpose for their lives set and established by God. Every child is born with a specific "Sound" that they are tuned to from the time your Father God created them as a flesh bound spirit at the moment of conception. You may understand what I am saying if I put it this way; everyone dances to a different beat, and like beats will attract to form the "Sound" that they were uniquely created from. Some family chords fit very well together and make a beautiful arrangement and that arrangement seems to move fluidly across the generations. Other family chords will have an off-beat member, section, or arrangement that just doesn't seem to match with the other musical notes and instruments being played, however, both were created as the "New Song" that we all will sing.

When the Lord gives you an assignment, often times your response might be much like mine was: "Ok, Lord, you have given me the Title "A Life of Significance", now what is it supposed to be about?" He answers, "I want you to write your life experiences." I said, "Ok, well that is only about a chapter or two, and that doesn't make a book, so what am I supposed to fill the pages with?" His final response was you have lots of friends, with stories to share, have them tell you their stories and incorporate them into the missing chapters." He didn't say exactly when this book was to be published, but I seemed to have June in my brain for some reason or another. Therefore, I naturally thought well, June 2011 it is, and not another word did He or has He spoken about the assignment that he has now given me. Now this conversation was taking place in July 2010, and I set out on my assignment to write this book. I sent out a post on my Facebook page saying; I am working on a new book, the working title is "A Life of Significance" and I was looking for others personal stories to combine into this book, and how each of these lives were significant. Regardless of how long or short their life was allows us to share those lives and show how those significant lives influenced them and the people around them. Much to my surprise, I had several people willing to share their stories with me, and each story contained valuable life lessons for all of us to glean.

Suddenly, November of 2010, my book comes to a grinding halt, I can't seem to write another word, some of the people that said that they want to share their stories, or assist with the book, seemed to be mysteriously quiet, and my book has now stalled. As any child of a parent knows when the parent is "up-to-something". I knew that God was working on all sides of this miracle called my first book. I knew that this was just a Divine Parental Delay of my

Daddy God. I knew that when it was time, He would have me resume writing, and all would be in His perfect timing.

Again, just has suddenly as the book had stalled in November 2010, the sense of urgency to finish this book returned in July 2011, and this time was different. I can't tell you how, simply because I don't know how, but this publisher found me, and asked if I had a book that needed to be published that I should send a query letter to let them know what the book was about and they would be in contact with me. Now the interesting thing about this publisher was that they weren't like other publishers that I had heard of before they were actually willing to pay me to write my book, and were not in the business of having author's pay them to have their books published, which in these days and times is almost unheard of for unknown authors. One by one everyone that I had previously heard from willing to share their stories with me began setting appointments for me to interview them.

I had a friend that back in 2010 when I told her that the Lord had given me an assignment to write a book, she dismissed my comment. She somehow began acting as if, how was I going to write a book when I had all these other businesses that God had called me to build and run and also the ministry to run. Once the book writing and stories began coming in on the project, this same friend, when I tell her in July 2011 that I am writing a book, she seemed surprised. Suddenly she directs me to her cousin that has not only a perfect story for my book; actually, her cousin contributes three different stories for this book, in three different sections.

Another person connected to the first printing of my book; "A Life Of Significance" was a photographer that I met through some friends and began talking to her about a particular picture she had taken. The photographer admits that back in 2010, when I first inquired about using one of her photographs for the front cover of this books' first edition, she gracefully allowed that request to fall to the ground, because there was NO Way that she was going to have a picture of herself on the cover of a book. Then over the course of 4 or 5 months after my first request, the Lord began healing some deep-seated wounds from her past, and suddenly she is contacting me and allowing me to use her photograph for the cover, free of charge, no strings attached, and now no hesitation.

So you see, you are about to embark on a journey of not only gleaning the lessons from some very significant lives, but you will be embarking on a journey through a lesson on how, the God of the Universe has created each of us to be significant within our own spheres of influence. You don't have to be famous to have A Life of Significance you only have to be human. Through the ordinary lives portrayed within the pages of this book, you will find that you too have A Life of Significance. Every life is A Life of Significance; we just need to learn to find the Golden God Nuggets hidden deep within. Regardless of whether it is a long life or a life that was cut tragically short, all lives are significant to those connected to them, and have golden nuggets of significance to others willing to mine them out. Through this book you will find hope and healing for any situation that you may currently be experiencing, and will receive a deposit from every life portrayed within the pages.

Section I

Planned Arrivals

Psalm 139:13–18

For You formed my inward parts; You covered me in my mother's womb. I will praise You, for I am fearfully and wonderfully made; Marvelous are Your works, And that my soul knows very well. My frame was not hidden from You, When I was made in secret, And skillfully wrought in the lowest parts of the earth. Your eyes saw my substance, being yet unformed. And In Your book they all were written, The days fashioned for me, When as yet there were none of them. How precious also are Your thought to me O God! How great is the sum of them! If I should count them, they would be more in number than the sand; When I awake, I am still with You.

1

The Conception Of Life

PRIOR TO AND at the moment of conception, everyone is significant to our Heavenly Father. Let's first look at what the bible says about how you were created and who is responsible for making your life A Life of Significance. In Isaiah 44:24 "Thus says the LORD, your Redeemer, And He who formed you from the womb; I am the LORD, who makes all things, Who stretches out the heavens all alone, Who spreads abroad the earth by Myself." We also see in in Isaiah 43:21 the reason that you were created; "This people I have formed for Myself; They shall declare My Praise." It makes no difference whether you were planned; unplanned, aborted, or taken away prematurely every life is significant prior to your conception. God Himself tells you exactly what His thoughts and plans are for you in Jeremiah 29:11: For I know the thoughts that I think toward you, says the LORD, thoughts of peace and not of evil, to give you a future and a hope. In this chapter we will begin to look at the day of your conception. The moment that you began to grow into the life that you now live is significant, and the plans that were made for your arrival created you to be the significant person that you have become.

The day of your conception was a very active and full day in your life. The life of your biological parents combined to create the life that you now are living. Just think of the plans that were made prior to your conception. First, your Heavenly Father, God, planned and designed how you were to be created within a womb of life. Oh my…how that womb was designed specifically to protect and feed you for the first nine months of your life, as you grew and developed. How your biological parents either knew that they wanted to create a child from their union, or you would be a complete surprise to them a few weeks later, all of that did not matter to the creator, Father God, His plans were made prior to your arrival as the significant person you were to become. Think about it, from the moments just prior to your conception let's look at all the plans and preparation that went into your arrival here on Earth. Your mother's body had to be perfectly designed to receive the sperm that was to penetrate the egg that she carried you in. Then the chain reaction and activity began, your cells began to multiply, and divide at an enormous rate to create every part of your body. Then it took nine months for you to become fully developed into a child that could stand the world into which you would be ushered. All of this took planning and preparation not on your parents part yet, but on your Heavenly Father's part. Now this should be beginning to show just how much you were expected and prepared for by your Heavenly Father, God. Now let's begin to look at what your parents did in preparation for your arrival.

Normally the first one to know of your existence is your mother. She begins to feel changes taking place in her body that she may or may not know what is causing them; hormonal changes are reacting and preparing to care for you deep within her womb. Her body is a complete orchestra playing just for you as you grow and develop. God planned and prepared her body just to be able to care for you prior to your birth, and the changes to her body at this point can only be felt or noticed by her and a medical doctor to confirm your existence! Once she became aware of you, she started making decisions, how will she care for you, what will she name you, the list is endless but very real and very intentional. Then she tells your dad of your existence, and he begins the same millions of decisions and questions about your future…where will you go to school, where will you sleep, how will he feed you etc… See you have already become SIGNIFICANT to at least two people and your Heavenly Father. Wow, and you haven't even made it onto the scene of your life yet, and already you are living A Life of Significance.

2

Marcus The Sole Survivor

Marcus my youngest of 7 children was the one that I was almost breathless with anticipation for. You see, just 6 weeks prior to me conceiving Marcus, I had a tubal pregnancy, with a tubal pregnancy you must undergo removal of the fetus from your fallopian tube or it will rupture and the mother and baby are put into certain danger. This is where the egg gets fertilized in the tube instead of the uterus. After the surgery, I was very upset and discouraged, but the Dr. told me that since he cleaned me all out, that he could almost guarantee that I would be pregnant again within 6 weeks. Sure enough, 6 weeks to the day, I was now pregnant with Marcus. Looking back now, I don't think that I would have appreciated him as much if I hadn't had the miscarriage of that significant life of my unborn child and the subsequent DNC and tube flushing just 6 weeks before. So right here, you can see what a significant life was of my unborn child that had to be removed, and I will share that story in a later chapter.

The night of Marcus' conception: I won't be getting graphic here but I do feel that it's important to share that the night that I conceived Marcus, we immediately knew I was incubating, because my body temperature rose dramatically, to the point that I was pouring sweat from every pore of my body in my sleep. My husband at the time said that I was sweating so profusely in my sleep that he had to get some towels and dry me off just so he could sleep. I was incubating! The next morning, I could almost feel the new life inside me. Not that you're supposed to this quickly, I just think that it was God's way of letting me know that Marcus was now being developed, and to get me ready for his arrival in 9 months. After a couple of months, my body began to reject the baby (Marcus) as a foreign object, and so I was every few days in and out of the hospital for the duration of my pregnancy. It was a long hard nine months, and I would continually talk to him, and tell him everything would be ok. I think I did this more for myself than I did for him. Somehow, I think he knew that he would be born soon and all the fuss over his development would soon be over.

The day of his birth finally came on October 16 that year, and my adorable son Marcus was born by C-Section. C-Section babies are so pretty since they don't have to go through all the trauma of being born the natural way, however, at times I wish that I could have given birth the normal way, because I do miss not having that experience. He was completcly beautiful, with ten fingers and ten little toes, and seemed to beam with excitement about his new life. He was such a good baby and also a very needy baby, wanting all my focus and attention 24 hours a day 7 days a week. Not that I minded, I just say that I was pregnant with him twice, nine months in the womb and for the first nine months of his life he had to eat round the clock every two hours from the beginning of the bottle, not the end of the bottle. Needless to say, I didn't get much sleep for the first nine months of his life, and he sure did enjoy the attention. I believe this is what caused our bond to be so close throughout all these years. My marriage to his biological father ended shortly thereafter, and we were on our own until one day I met the man that he now calls Dad. His Dad seemed to take an instant attachment to him, and they grew to be the best father/son team that I know. Marcus intently watched everything that his dad did, sometimes to the point of making his dad nervous. His dad would tell me in private, "He's always watching me and it makes me nervous". As Marcus grew up, the two were inseparable, and his dad learned that if something ever happened to me, that Marcus would be taken away to a family that he didn't know. The laws in the State of Texas are that if a child's custodial parent dies, that child is then removed from the Step-Parent home and sent to live with the other biological parent regardless of whether that parent has seen them in years or not. This is why his dad decided that he wanted to adopt him, because he didn't want Marcus to have to go live with a family that he never knew and away from his older brother that was still living at home, and the other children of the family.

Marcus is our adrenaline junkie. He knew NO FEAR growing up, and all he knew was go faster and go harder. So it was no surprise to us when he was 19 years old that he decided to join the Army and be all he could be, and see all he could see. Not a decision that I was too terribly happy with, but it was his decision and his dad and I stood behind him. At Marcus' graduation ceremony from boot camp, the sergeant told all of us parents to look around the room and to please know that 50% or more of these young men and women would not come back from the war for which they were being sent. He called this group a "Crazy Bunch" but a "Crazy Bunch" that he was honored to know and serve with. A very sobering thought, and not one that I really wanted to remember as Marcus left for Iraq just 14 days prior to his birthday that year, as a matter of fact, he celebrated his 20 birthday in Southern Baghdad, Iraq. We heard from him almost every day by text message, which made it easier to deal with, except when December came, and word stopped coming. It was the longest two weeks I believe his dad and I ever spent during his tour. Then, the week of Christmas he called from Germany telling us that he was E-Vac'd out of Baghdad, but that he was OK. How can you be OK if you were sent by medical helicopter from a Baghdad hospital to the hospital in Germany just didn't make sense, but we were glad to finally hear from him. Five men in his squad had been killed in an ambush that day in Iraq, and if it hadn't been for the Special Forces team, Marcus would have been number 6; however, he was only slightly injured in the attack. Christmas Eve he finally arrived back at his home base at Fort Hood, Texas, and I think that was the most emotional Christmas I have ever had. You see, he spent the next week at the hospital in Fort Hood trying to convince them that he was not crazy just because he believed that Jesus Christ died on the cross and rose on the third day. This was Christmas Eve, and as his dad and I were on the phone with him that evening, I heard a nurse's voice talking to Marcus asking him if he was angry at everyone that didn't believe that Jesus Christ died on a Cross was buried and rose on the third day?" Marcus' response was "No, I don't understand people that don't believe that my Lord and Savior died on a Cross and rose on the third day, but believing in Jesus doesn't make me crazy either." His dad with his quick wit immediately told Marcus tell all those people "Well, you all are expecting a Fat Man in a Red suit to come down your chimney tonight, now who is the Crazy is one?" What a testimony, and what a Significant Life, to be able to testify of his Lord and Savior to so many people. Now remember what the sergeant at graduation told us about how many would not come back from the war? Of his squad that he graduated with from boot camp he is the sole survivor of his squad, so please remember all our men and women in combat across the world. All gave some, and some gave ALL! Marcus is now married to a beautiful woman and has two beautiful boys, Jacob and Lucas, carrying on that significant life for many generations to come!

3

Keagan's Prophetic Entrance

I FIRST MET Tommy and Karen while they were serving as Youth Pastors at the church we all attended in Decatur, Texas and Keagan was about 4 or 5 at the time. Over the years, we became co-workers together, them as the Youth Pastors and I as the Children's Pastor. I had their son Keagan in my Children's group, and I was so taken by him and his parents. Keagan showed a tremendous love of God, and has a tremendous love for people. Over the course of our working together, Tommy and Karen had shared bits and pieces of their story about how Keagan came into their life, and as I began, working on this book Karen offered her assistance anyway that she could. The further the book got, and no word from Karen as to anything that she had come up with to share, I began to pray about her contribution. Suddenly, like a rock flying in the air, it hit me; ask her if she would share Keagan's arrival and later you will see why

I titled this chapter Keagan's Prophetic Arrival. She was thrilled to help, and excited that she had a story to share. I was pleased that she shared Keagan's story.

Karen said that she would "never forget the night their life would change forever. It was November 1995 in Monroe, Louisiana listening to a friend of ours preaching when my husband of 13 years leaned over and said to me "we should have another baby". MY husband , the father of our handsome 12 year old son and gorgeous 10 year old daughter suggesting out of the blue that we should have another child! He must have fallen on his head! My response was quick and curt "Dear I will need a flying frying pan from Heaven to knock me in the head as a SIGN that we are to have another child!""

Tommy and Karen's lives were busy, both of them working 60 hours a week as Youth Pastors. They had a youth church of nearly 100 and they barely had time to love all those kids AND raise the two of their own that they had, let alone add a third to the mix and a NEWBORN at that, the discussion was closed as far as Karen was concerned! The next day was Sunday and as was their usual routine, they headed off early in the morning to church, not a word of another baby between them or with anyone else for that matter. During the sermon their pastor a fiery and determined preacher that never takes "rabbit trails" in his sermons, STOPS out of the blue and takes a side bar by saying "Oh and by the way, YOU don't need a SIGN from Heaven to have another baby, your quiver is not full until 5." Then the pastor continues with his sermon of the day. Time stood still for Tommy and Karen. They looked at each other, wide eyed and "with wonder, but I think it was more SHOCK." They mouthed at each other saying, "Did we just hear that correctly?" "Was that not a clear sign?" they said together in whispered unison! Karen's head was screaming "My Lord, WHY, WHY would you want ME to have another baby? Lord if a special child is to be born in this world please don't give them to ME, I will mess them up!" Then came the expected questions, "Why us? Why now?" As the questions continued rolling on the "sign" was clear, the Word was plain, clear, and actually quite loud. They were to have another child and they would have to make a choice as to whether they walked toward this calling, or continued into their own plans.

Karen began with all the excuses that she could come up with "I'm old (32yrs old at the time) I'm overweight, I shouldn't be having a baby. I've been on the pill for 10 years, I probably can't get pregnant." Just so happens that her yearly gynecological visit was already scheduled, and was only a week away, so Karen thought, who better to consult with than my doctor. Much to Karen's surprise or maybe even dismay or bewilderment, she was told that she was NOT too old, NOT too overweight or had she been on birth control too long to have a baby. Her doctor did give her some advice such as to get off the pill, wait three months and then try. At this point Karen's head is spinning and she is thinking, "This is all too surreal. Could this really be happening?"

As there "is wisdom in the counsel of many", they decided to tell their two children, her parents and their pastor of this life changing decision. The replies were unanimous and exactly how they were feeling "ARE YALL CRAZY?" The kids actually were a bit excited, but when presented with "the sign" their pastor insisted that he had never preached what we had heard that Sunday morning during his sermon. Karen, being the person that rarely could accept "your wrong" for an answer went back and listened to that Sunday's message, and then every message from the whole month, and then every message from the three consecutive months… "I was going to find it and prove to him that he did to say it!" Karen was never able to find the recording on any tape. They were in awe that God would do such a supernatural intervention into their lives to give them the sign they needed for His plan, and had delivered personally just to them. "God's direction and counsel is our final authority in the end and we chose to follow what we knew we had experienced."

They already had their minds made up on what gender of child they wanted. Through this process, God was going to set Karen free from years of engrained family traditions that had held her hostage for so long. Since this was all walking by pure faith they decided they wanted to choose the gender of their child to be a girl. In December of 1995, Karen purchased the book; How To Choose The Sex Of Your Baby which is based upon the bodies chemical makeup, and timing and she believed that her and Tommy could actually "Order Up" the child that God wanted them to have! Therefore, for the next seven months Karen tracked her cycles paying attention to all the signs of ovulation and planning when they should conceive to have their best chances for a girl. Through this process, Tommy and Karen knowing all they knew to do would continually pray over their bodies and the future child. They were claiming all the scriptures that they could during this time, and they truly believed that God would give them the desires of their hearts, since they were being obedient to have the child that God had instructed them to have.

On July 10, 1996, Tommy and Karen celebrated their 14th wedding anniversary. They had a great day together and enjoyed being more in love with each other than when they were first married. A couple of days later, Karen said, "I had all the symptoms of ovulation; the timing was perfect for a girl! I ran in to Tommy, we laid hands on my abdomen, and we prayed believing we would be conceiving our girl, commanding our little girl sperm to swim, swim, swim"! I must say the next few weeks were the longest ever, wondering if we had our itty-bitty baby growing inside of me. We prayed over my womb everyday with expectant hope that our baby was developing and on the way." Karen, being the; I want to know now type of person, just had to set out and purchase her first, of many pregnancy tests. Usually you need to wait at least a few days after your missed cycle, but Karen's impatience got the better of her. After arriving home with her first test, she was sure that she saw a little pink line on the stick. She immediately called Tommy at the office and told him that she had purchased a pregnancy test, and it was faint, but there was in fact a little pink line, and in a typical "man" voice, "He laughed and said you really should have waited" but he too was excited over the news that their baby was in the making. Tommy and Karen waited until they had taken 16 more pregnancy tests, all confirming the positive result of the first one before they told the other kids, they were ecstatic!

During Karen's first OB visit, there was a scare due to the heartbeat not being found. She was to return to the doctor's office later in the day for an ultrasound. She and Tommy began an extra prayer vigil, again laying hands on her belly, and commanding life to remain, for the child to be strong and not come forth until its time. The ultrasound found a good strong heartbeat with no problems. The pregnancy went well with just a little morning sickness, which was a miracle to Karen, as she had been ill 24/7, and in and out of the hospital with the first two. So began the parade of baby stuff; Pink, Pink and More Pink, bows and headbands, lace and frills, there was in their minds no doubt that they were expecting the arrival of the little girl that they had requested/ordered up.

December 19th is the day that they will never forget their scheduled ultrasound. Soon Tommy and Karen would learn and get to see their little girl for the first time. Karen with a full bladder Tommy right by her side and their little girl waiting to make her debut onto the scene of Tommy and Karen's perfect little family. As they all stood around in the dark room while the ultrasound film to be developed, the news is announced "It's a Boy". Karen, not one to take "No" or to have someone disagrees with what SHE knows or thinks she knows asks, "What? Are you sure? You must be mistaken, I am having a little girl, I have already bought all the little girl things, and everything is set for our little girl. Please look again. The reply is the same, "No Mrs. Lee, it's for sure a little boy". The silence was deafening as they left the hospital that day.

Later that afternoon, they arrived back at the church to put food baskets together. There was complete and utter silence with only the shuffling of food being placed into baskets for the soon arrival of people who were in need of their assistance. No one in the room knew or dared say anything to Karen, because when Karen is proved wrong, and should anyone confront her while she is still processing the new information, she will fall apart in shock, disbelief and maybe even a little grief for a while, as she get acclimated to the "New Truth", that they are having a little boy!

So begins, the God and Faith interrogation: What happened to all those prayers? What happened to that desires of our heart business? Karen had been so worked up over the "new information" that they were having a little boy, she just simply couldn't or should I say didn't need to be around people at this point. This was something that Karen would have to work out just between her and God, and an audience is never a good thing when questioning our heavenly Father! Upon arriving home all Karen saw was a sea of PINK, and here came the water works, and more questioning; "God what are you thinking? I had this baby for YOU, shouldn't I at least get the one I want!" Therefore, the pity party continued for 3-1/2 hours, crying, questioning, and probably a little loud discussing.

A dear friend of Tommy and Karen's named Tina inquired of Tommy, who if you remember is right where Karen had left him to have her private pity party, still at the church filling food baskets, and Tommy proceeded to tell her the "New News" that they were having a BOY. Now we girls know when our closest girlfriends get hold of us while we are trying to have our own little pity party, we don't get to remain long in our wallowing. I am convinced that friends are just Angels only without the wings! Tina immediately gets on the phone, and interrupts Karen's pity party. "Karen, get your butt up to your office and I will meet you there!" Upon Karen's arrival to her office there waiting was Tina and the 3 largest black bags of little boy stuff that she had ever seen. Inside each bag was the best of the best that you could ever want or need for your new little boy's arrival. Karen began going through each piece within each bag and her disappointment and sadness of losing the little girl that never was seemed to melt away. As each thread of disappointment disappeared, the Lord seemed to replace it with extreme joy over their new little boy who would soon arrive and be named Keagan John Paul Lee. On March 21, 1997 at 11:35 a.m. after being in labor for 5 ½ hours their beautiful and perfect baby boy arrived.

Later that day, Tommy and Karen receive a call from their pastor's brother, Steve, who lives in Ohio with congratulations and a request for an apology. As it seems, and they had all but forgotten that in March of 1990, Steve a pastor and prophet had visited their church. During his visit, she and Tommy had gone up for prayer where Steve had spoken a Word from the Lord over Karen. "I see a blessing of the womb," says Steve, "OH NO YOU DON'T!" was Tommy's partial response as he stepped between Steve and Karen as if the very words spoken would impregnate her. "You need to look again; we don't want or need no blessings of the womb!" Tommy finished as Steve stumbled on "yes yes a blessing of the womb… spiritual womb, blessing of spiritual children". Seven years to the month the prophecy was fulfilled. To add to the prophetic arrival of Keagan, within spiritual understanding the number seven is God's number for completion.

As the years go by Keagan's prophetic arrival, takes on new and deeper meaning for Tommy and Karen. The biggest was that God wanted the "curse" of wanting girls to be broken off their family! This is actually called the "curse" of desiring a matriarchal society in which the women rule and basically castrate their husband's authority within the family unit. This was actually the "Sin" that Satan introduced into the Garden of Eden when that old devil, the serpent convinced Eve to go against what her husband Adam and God had discussed about not partaking of the forbidden fruit.

The other dimensions to Keagan's prophetic arrival came within the first 18 months of his life. Tommy and Karen were called to plant a church over 3000 miles away from their family and friends. These were dark and lonely times for their entire family, which I believe has melding them into one of the strongest families that I have had the privilege to know. We all know that having an 18 month old can definitely add spice and fun into your life, as well as occupy your brains to the point that you don't realize that you are actually away from your family and loved ones. Keagan was that bright spot for them that got them though the midnight hours of building a church from the ground up!

Then again in 2006 when Keagan was 9 years old Tommy and Karen were called to move to England. There again Keagan's prophetic arrival provided them the much needed boost of faith and helped them maintain a positive outlook on their circumstances. Karen recalls that first Christmas without their two oldest children, that couldn't make the journey with them to England, nor did God provide a way for them to visit during the holidays, Keagan was in their words, "Their salvation". Karen said, "We had to put our focus on him, and not give into the temptation of depression that assailed us from not being with the rest of our family during the holidays. Keagan kept us busy with his Christmas spirit and full of hope with his love for people and us. Keagan John Paul Lee is a blessing and joy that is beyond imagination! We cannot fathom our lives without him! When we meet new people who ask, "Do you have children", and their response to our "yes we have a 28, 26 and 14 year old" is "OH a late in life surprise" we are so PROUD to say "NO, our late in life greatest decision! Our first two were "our oops" and Gods plan, and Keagan is our God's plan and our obedience!""

#1 Points To Ponder

Highlights from the previous chapters shows that you were no accident. You were uniquely formed, expected and planned for by your Heavenly Father. He also admired before you existed in your earth suit. Your parents, regardless of whether they realized it or not, planned for your arrival by the internal parental code placed within them by God. Every creature created by God has this internal parental code placed within them, and if you don't believe that sit back and watch nature for a while. The birds build nests in preparation for the arrival of their offspring, a dog or cat when time comes close to their young being born will find a suitable bed, and expectant mothers go through the nesting process weeks in advance of their baby's arrival. Parental instincts are as natural as breathing.

Our men and women who are serving in our Armed Forces for our country are first and foremost on assignment from God. God is the one who has placed within them the desire to protect their God given country, regardless of what country that they may live in. Throughout the bible we find that it is a great honor to serve ones country, in defense of that country. We aren't going to get into the argument of who is right and who is wrong, simply the fact that God has placed each individual in their own country, and gives certain individuals a clear mandate from Heaven to serve and protect their country and their fellow citizens.

When one stands for Jesus, no foe can stand against them. Jesus called each of us to be witnesses for Him in whatever situation that we find ourselves in, and we have seen a clear example of that. Regardless of whether the other people involved acknowledge or follow Christ that is not our concern, our concern is that we acknowledge Him before men, and He will acknowledge us before God and all of Heaven. The bible clearly shows us that to accept the Son, we gain the Father also. I am reminded of a story about a certain rich man that had an only son. That son died while serving in a time of war, and the father was somehow consoled by the only painting that he had of his son. One day the old man died, not leaving any heirs to his vast estate. When his items were sent to the auction house, the instructions in the old man's will said that the first thing that was to be sold was this one painting. All of the man's possessions were placed on exhibit, however, when time for the auction to begin, the auctioneer was only allowed to auction the painting first and it had to sell first. The crowd was outraged, you see, the painting wasn't a very good painting, however the auctioneer had to abide by the wishes set forth in the old man's will. The auctioneer, started the bidding at $100.00 and nobody would even cast their bid, finally the auctioneer asked if any would bid $50.00 for this painting and still no takers, and frustrated with the crowd yelling to place the other items up for sale instead of this old painting, the auctioneer said, ok, will anybody give me $5.00 for this painting to that we can move on with this sale. Finally, a little old woman, stood up and said, Yes, I will bid $5.00 dollars for that painting, and suddenly, the crowd went wild, and the auctioneer sighed a sigh of relief that finally they could get on with the sale of the other items. The auctioneer, said going once, going twice, SOLD to the little woman in the corner. Now unknown to the auctioneer, there was a letter attached to the sale of the painting, and in that letter it said, "To the person that purchased this favorite painting of my son, I give you all of my possessions and nothing more is available to be sold because it all belongs now to the new owner of the painting of My Son." Moral of the story is: He who takes the Son gains it all.

Many times when God speaks to us, we fail to hear him, because he speaks in a still small voice and is never pushy or rude. Many times His voice can sound so real like someone had just said something to us, and we have to wonder, who was talking to us, or ask ourselves did I really just hear what I heard. Regardless of whether anyone else heard what God may have spoken to you, He still speaks, and will never tell you anything that goes against His word or His commandments, and if He says something, we should pay more earnest heed to the things that He speaks, because He only wants what is best for each of us as His children. Sometimes people confuse the harsh God of the Old Testament of the Bible with the New Testament God who is not mad at His children any longer. Jesus paid the price that was owed for our sins of rejecting Him, and all we must do is accept the Son and we gain true Life, and everything God and Heaven have to offer.

In the following chapters, we will learn that God spoke of his Son many times to man, and man failed to understand what God was talking about. However, this didn't stop the plan of God for giving his only begotten Son to us to pay the price for our freedom from the bondages of sin. However, had Jesus not submitted to the Plan of God for his life, we would still be looking for a savior to save us from our sinful ways. God always has His part in our lives, and we have our free will to choose our part in our lives. The choice is clear, God will always do His part will we do our part in His plan for our life? Many times where we fail to accomplish what God's plans are for our lives, is when we don't couple the Mercy of God with His truth that he has spoken in his word regarding our situations. Without the Mercy of God we become controlling dictators beating up everyone around us with the Truth of God, and without His Truth given to us in His Word, we get chewed up by others taking advantage of our God given Mercy.

Section II

Unexpected Blessings

Jeremiah 1:5–10

"Before I formed you in the womb I knew you; Before you were born I sanctified you; I ordained you a prophet to the nations." Then said I: "Ah, Lord GOD! Behold, I cannot speak, for I am a youth." But the LORD said to me: "Do not say, 'I am a youth,' For you shall go to all to whom I send you, And whatever I command you, you shall speak. Do not be afraid of their faces, For I am with you to deliver you," says the LORD. The LORD put forth His hand and touched my mouth and the LORD said to me; "Behold, I have put My words in your mouth. See, I this day set you over the nations and over the kingdoms, To root out and to pull down, To destroy and to throw down, to build and plant."

4

Jesus – Prophesied About But Still Unexpected

MARY AND JOSEPH were you average young couple living in Israel many years ago. Mary a young girl and Joseph a man just wanting to start a family and go about his job as the village carpenter. Back then, the man would ask a young woman to marry him, and then he would leave and begin getting everything together for his young bride. He had to build the house, and get furnishing put into place, and then gets his father's approval that everything was ready to accept his new bride. Mary in the meantime, waiting for the time that all the preparation were ready, and almost breathless in anticipation of her wedding day, gathered herself her belongings, and groomed herself in preparation of the big day, waiting for her groom to return and tell her that everything was ready for her arrival. Now, unknown to Mary and Joseph, Father God had different plans of his own. Late one night, an angel of the Lord came to call on Mary, and told her that she would become pregnant with God's Son, and that she shouldn't be afraid. Now, the first thing is Mary had to be accustom to receiving angels, because the angel didn't frighten her, what confused her was his words that she would become pregnant without having known a man. After the angel left, is when Mary become frightened, how was she going to tell her fiancé, and what would be his reaction. In those days, girls who were unfaithful to their husbands caused quite a stir in their small villages, and were marked for life for the unfaithfulness. The time comes that Joseph comes to tell her that all the preparation were made, and ready to receive her as his wife, but much to his surprise, she has news of her own.

Mary tells Joseph of the angels' visit, and that she is now pregnant with God's child, and she watches as Josephs' heart sank. Now what was he to do, the woman that he is to marry is pregnant, and she swears that she has not known a man in the sexual sense, but she is pregnant with God's child. Joseph leaves to consider what he is to do now, he still loves Mary, and wishes no harm to come to her, but he knows that if he divorces her, everyone in the village will know soon why they divorced and she will become the village tramp, and exiled from village life. So that night as he is dealing with what Mary told him, an angel visits him, and tells him that he is to take Mary as his wife, just as he planned, and that she would indeed give birth to a child, and he was to call the child's name Jesus. The next morning Joseph arrives at Mary's home and takes her to be his wife, and begins to show her everything that he had prepared for her as his wife. Joseph explains that he too had a visit from an angel and that the angel indeed told him that all was ok, she had been a faithful fiancée to him, and that she would give birth to the Son of God, and they were to name him Jesus. Mary breathed a sigh of relief, knowing that Joseph had just protected her and her child from ridicule of the village, and that all would be ok. Only Mary and Joseph would know that the child wasn't Joseph's but was God's Son. Mary goes to visit her cousin Elizabeth, knowing that she would soon deliver her son and Mary wanted to be with her to help with the newborn. As soon as Elizabeth opened the door to receive Mary into her home, Elizabeth screams with excitement because John leaps when Mary and her unborn child, Jesus walk-in and Elizabeth exclaims that Mary was the mother of our Lord. Well, so much for no one knowing about the baby, the proverbial cat is out of the bag now.

After Mary returns home from her visit, it is almost time for their annual visit to Jerusalem to pay their tributes and taxes, and attend the annual feast. Along the way, Mary goes into labor and Joseph has to find a place for Mary to give birth. Every hotel and motel was filled to capacity, and there wasn't a room to be had. Mary tells Joseph, enough already, just make me a bed in that old barn in the haystack and I will deliver the child there. Literally, Jesus was born in a barn, no fanfare, no bed for his mother, nothing! Joseph takes care of the business in Jerusalem, and they are getting ready to leave to go back home. That night Joseph has a dream and an angel of the Lord tells him that people are seeking to kill the child, and that he needs to get up and get the mother and child out of there as soon as possible and to take a different route home.

Joseph and Mary keep the child safe for many years to come, moving about as the Lord directs them through his angels, until one day, they no longer move around. Joseph had died several years prior, and it is just Mary, Jesus, and his brothers carrying on the family carpentry business. Mary listened to every word that Jesus would say, knowing that he was the Son of God, and she knew that he was destined for greatness, but not knowing that his greatness would cost him is life.

At age 33-1/2 years of age, Jesus hung on a cross and died, for all the sins of mankind. Moreover, on the third day rose again from the grave, so that all of mankind was now set free from their sinful nature if they would only believe upon him as the Son of God, who came to save them from their sin. Such a short life and an unselfish life to redeem sinful man back to God himself, what A Life of Significance, and the greatest sacrifice that would ever be made for you and I.

5

John And His Halo!

This story is a story of how the unexpected life of John, the youngest child of Shelly and Rickey, miraculously ushered life into their dying relationship. Shelly and Rickey had been married for 7 years, and this was their second attempt at trying to make their marriage work. At the time, they had two children ages five and twelve, and they were on the brink of another separation. Rickey was an alcoholic, and Shelly was walking through life with a very large chip on her shoulder, taking her lot in life out on everyone she could. The kids were a wreck, and the seven years had taken its toll on all of them. The only light at the end of the tunnel for Shelly was that both kids would soon be in school the upcoming year, and she could go back to school herself, to be able to support her and the kids for what was to come.

Shelly knew that what was coming was another end to hers and Rickey's marriage and she was attempting to start putting the pieces of her life together without Rickey in it. She knew that at her current education level she would never be able to support herself and the kids. Shelly also believed that getting a better education would also give her a greater sense of accomplishment and self-worth that she had not felt in a very long time. Three days after Rickey and Shelly discussed a final separation, Shelly found out that she was again pregnant, and all of Shelly's plans had somehow been thwarted once again, which devastated her. Her emotions ran the gauntlet that her plans of having a better life had been messed up by this unexpected pregnancy. Rickey and Shelly decided to postpone the separation until the baby was born. The entire nine months, she just seemed to be going through the motion of life, and trying to prepare for the new arrival. She tried to make herself happy about the situation, however when anyone would ask her about her pregnancy, she answered always in a negative tone, and in her words "was not a beaming mother to be, and wallowed in self-pity" and "now all of my plans that I had were down the toilet."

John's birthday finally came, and it was a very long labor ending with John being stuck in the birth canal. After nine hours of hard labor and the doctor attempting to use a suction cup several times to assist in his delivery, John couldn't make his way out and had to be born by an emergency C-Section. Shelly was only allowed to see John for a short second before he was rushed out of the operating room. As Shelly lay on the operating room table, she could tell by the doctors' and nurses working in a hurried pace and how white Rickey was that something was terribly wrong. Shelly was taken to the ICU to be monitored for a while, she vaguely remembers her family, and friends coming in and telling her to be strong, and that John was going to be ok. At this point, she still had no idea of exactly what was wrong with him. Two hours later, she was taken back to her room and their pediatrician came in to talk to them, and provided some more details on John's condition. He explained the seriousness of John's injuries and that Cooks Children's Hospital Care Flight helicopter was in route to take him to their facilities. John was born with a skull fracture, a large hematoma from the suction cup, and fluid in his skull cavity, blood was seeping onto his brain, and his blood platelet count was dropping rapidly. The pediatrician then escorted Rickey to NICU to see John before he left for Children's Hospital, and when he came back into Shelly's room, he was crying and very upset.

Shelly demanded to see John since she had only seen him for a few short seconds after his birth. "When he was in my arms I gently took off the little hat that was on his head and I literally couldn't breathe, his little head was so swollen and purple, and I could see the fluid moving around his face and neck." After only five minutes with him, the Care Flight team walked in with an incubator to transport him to Cook's Children Hospital and that would be that last time for three entire days that Shelly would see her newborn son. Rickey followed John to Cook's Hospital leaving Shelly all alone that first night. She couldn't sleep, and all she could keep thinking about was how selfish she had been the last nine months. "All I had done was complaining about how this baby had ruined My Plans and My Dreams. I cried and cried-out of fear, out of guilt and out of love for my son. I prayed all night for God's forgiveness, and I prayed for John's healing."

After only six days at Cooks hospital, and many visits from specialists and neurologists, they were finally able to take John home, and were told that it "did not appear that John would have any long term damage from his injuries". It did take five month for his head to completely heal and for the swelling to go down and the fluid to dissipate, but eventually John was completely healed, and whole. John is almost 10 now, and he is a normal, rambunctious boy who has a perfect circular scar on the top of his head from the suction cup, which they call his halo!

When asked about how their ideals and expectations in their marriage had grown and changed since John's birth, the following is what Shelly said: "I think John being born with his problems was a wakeup call to both Rickey and I. We had never had to face the possibly of having a child die or ending up with brain damage. We both realized that there was more to our life than our own personal issues. Rickey and I did eventually separate and it was during the time that Rickey's alcoholism reached its highest point. Then on his own, he decided that enough was enough, he joined AA and got himself into counseling. Through all this, watching Joel Osteen on TV, reading his books, and visiting a church, he renewed his faith in God and began to make his way back to the beliefs that he had had as a child. Neither the kids nor Shelly played any part in his recovery; it was all Rickey and ALL GOD! When Rickey first started his recovery, he told Shelly what he was doing and she supported him but did not interfere. "I did not run back to him or baby him in any way. I had a strong, strong feeling from God that I needed to stay out of it, so I did. It was very, very hard not to go to him in the moments he was going through withdraws and serious bouts of depression, but I just felt so strongly that I needed to let him go through it alone. I know in my heart that is when God was working with Rickey the most, and that his direction and focus needed to be on God and not on me. Rickey and I have talked about it many times since then and he said that if I had come running to him to help him he probably wouldn't be where he is today. He has not had one drop in four almost five years now. We can now talk openly of God, our faith, we all go to church and are very happy now." "The biggest change in me is that I no longer care what others think about me, I only care what God thinks of me. HE knows who I am and what I am, and He knows the truth. I cannot control how others act and feel, but I can control how I act and how I feel. My attitude is different in the fact that I wake up every morning thankful, and grateful for everything I have in my life, the good, the bad, and the ugly. I also know that things happen in our life that we may not like or understand at the time, but there is a reason for it and things don't always happen on our timetable. We have to be patient and wait for God's timing!" Shelly no longer walks around with a chip on her shoulder thinking that her life is so bad. She has a lot more respect for people and their feelings and she no longer takes her circumstances out on others as she did in the past."

Shelly and Rickey have been under the same roof now for five years now, and in Shelly's words, "It has been absolutely wonderful! I did get to go back to school and became a Surgical Assistant. Every time I was in the OR on a C-Section I got a big lump in my throat when the baby was delivered and I would have to force myself not to cry". We should all realize and remember that our life is only 20% of what happens to us and 80% of how we respond to our trials and life issues.

6

Sasha Our Minister Of Mercy

Now I DON'T know if this story will seem logical to you, but have you ever met a logical thinking 19 year old? However, this is a story that I believe needs to be told since so many other girls out there may have given up their children for adoption, and listened to the lies that are often surrounding them. I was 19 years old, and desperate to get out of my parent's home, for the second time. Moreover, I really didn't care how I got out but all I wanted was OUT! Five months back in their house was miserable, and I needed to get out before I went insane. I met a man eleven years older than I was, and a Vietnam War Veteran, which gave me an education like the one I had never had before. This man offered me an opportunity to get out of my parent's house and I took it, not knowing that we would live with different friends of his for the first couple of months, or at people's houses where a party had been the night before, and we would simply crash there for the night, never having our own place to sleep.

After a couple of months of this, we finally were able to get into our own apartment and begin living our life, such as it was. Now, I was just recently coming from a very depressed state after having to give up my son for adoption. The current stories that were running around the home for unwed mothers was that if you had to be put to sleep during the birthing process that the doctors would tie your tubes to prevent you from having any more children. Now I know as a 50 years old woman, that this was just a gossip mill running ramped but at the time I wasn't sure if they did this or not since my son had to be delivered by emergency C-Section, so how I became pregnant with my daughter was more from just wanting to see if they had "fixed" me or not.

The end of August came, and we decided to get married over Labor Day weekend. A short time later, I learned that I was indeed pregnant, and you can't imagine the relief and excitement that I had learning that I was pregnant again. In fact, for the first couple of months, I would take a home pregnancy test every week, just to make sure that I was not dreaming. The thought that kept running through my head was, "I am pregnant and they can't take this one away from me!" Now, my mother-in-law at the time was GREAT, she was one of these coupon freaks, that saved coupons for everything, and she started gathering diapers for our new arrival to come in May. By the time Sasha was born, she had accumulated an entire hall closet full of disposable diapers, in all sizes, so that we wouldn't need to buy diapers for years it seemed. I truly believe that she is the one that taught me just how much money you could save by using the coupons that came in the newspapers every week.

Sasha was born May 13, 1982, and really, I almost named her "Rainy Day" because it had been raining for days that year, and the day that she was born was the rainiest day and had every freeway in town flooding so much that the doctor almost wasn't able to arrive at the hospital in time for my C-Section. Anyway, Sasha was perfectly formed but she didn't look like what I thought a cute little baby should look like, she looked like a little old man. She had snow-white hair and a wrinkled little face, she reminded me of a little old man, but I loved her more than words could express. Plans were that since I would need some help with the new baby, my mother-in-law insisted that we stay at their house for the first few weeks so that she could help with Sasha, and help change my bandages since she was an LVN at a local hospital. This was such a blessing, to have someone who wanted to help take care of me and the baby, she had no hidden agendas, just pure love and compassion for me, her son, and newest granddaughter and had she not insisted, I don't know what I would have done to get through those first few weeks.

Sasha was such a good little baby, she would have her last bottle around Midnight and wouldn't wake up again until 9 or 10 o'clock the next morning for her next feeding from minute one that we brought her home from the hospital. The nurses in the hospital had quite a different opinion of her, and would bring her into me in the middle of the night telling me, "well, she has done it again, cried and screamed until she got all of the other babies woken up in the nursery and she decides that it is time to go back to sleep, and left us with a crying nursery." She never did that when we got her home though, but this should have been our first clue, that she was going to be a handful. I left

Sasha's biological father after 6 months, due to situations that are not appropriate for this book.

As Sasha grew, I soon realized that she was a precocious little girl, and the world seemed to be at her disposal. There wasn't anything that Sasha couldn't do once she set her mind to it, and she definitely had a mind of her own from a very young age. I remember once she and I had gone out to dinner when she was about two years old as was our normal custom a couple of times a week. As we sat there deciding on what we were going to have at Red Lobster that night, I looked at her and said, "Now you are paying for this right?" and she said, "No, I don't got any money, you have money" and I looked at her and said, "I don't have any money to pay for this, what are we going to do?", she instantly said, "Let's go Momma, before they bring out the food". Well the gig is up, and I have to tell her that I was just playing with her, and the relief that came over her face was great, and one that I will never forget. Then she was angry with me for the rest of the meal for scaring her like that. Oh, well, my bad! Nevertheless, it was funny though, to see that her first response was to get out of there before the food came.

Soon, Sasha grew into a beautiful young woman, full of life, care and compassion for others that I had never seen anyone before. She always cares about the needs of others before herself, and sometimes as a Minister of Mercy, she places herself in dangerous or hazardous situations before she realizes it. She will take in any stray, whether it is human or animal and tries to love them back into a better situation than they were before. She has never met a stranger, and to this day, I don't know if she even knows what a stranger is. She has such a kind and merciful way about her, and she never judges anyone for anything that they may have done, she simply looks for ways to help them and at any expense to herself. I often wonder if our little Minister of Mercy was just being merciful on me as a new mom when she was sleeping through the night from the minute that we brought her home, and has provided us with four wonderful grandchildren, Taylor, Braeden, Alexis, and Aurora Grace, full of mercy and grace!

7

Johnathan's Touch – Part One

My life was filled with strings attached; however, little did I know the biggest string that would be attached would stick with me for the rest of my life. I had been waiting to start going to this club that all my friends had been going to for several months, the name of the club was Savvy's, however my family continually referred to it as "scabies", which if you know anything about kids exactly what you forbid them to do or speak ill about, is exactly what they are going to do. I was a rebellious child yes, however, not without a cause. You see, my family had my life all planned for me; I would grow up, become a major lawyer, and make them proud to be my family. Big mistake, parents don't plan your children's life out for them, they must search and seek out their own plans and destinies for themselves, and all you will do is alienate them from your life if you have your own agendas for their lives. Parents should prompt, guide, or even nudge but never force your will upon your children you will be highly disappointed in their reactions.

It is now my 18th birthday and I finally was able to go to the club that all my friends had been talking about. I met a man there who was a year older than I was, and we began to date steadily. I was now fixing to become my parent's worst nightmare, unmarried, and pregnant, and that was not in my parents plans at all for my life. It would several months before I would come to realize that I was pregnant, and high school graduation was just around the corner. My parents were so proud that I had finally graduated, I will admit it was a long junior and senior year and they couldn't wait for my college career to begin, which wasn't what I had planned. Graduation Night came and I had a curfew of Midnight, end of subject! So I was hell bent on moving out as soon as I could which would be the next morning.

I had a full-time job that I had gotten with an insurance company prior to graduation, and was gainfully employed. I moved in with some friends of mine the morning after graduation to wait for my apartment to be ready me to move into, and so began, life on my own. Oh, and the man that I had started dating from Savvy's was no longer in my life either, we had broken up a month before graduation, and I still didn't know that I was pregnant. So here I was, gainfully employed, single, and making a life of my own, until…July of that year. I began to have a little baby pooch, and then it hits me square in the face, I am pregnant and single. My thought was well, I have a good job, and we will just make the most of it, end of subject. Oh, how wrong I was. When I told my family that I was pregnant in a few short days they had everything all worked out, I would get rid of the baby by having an abortion at a clinic in California that was waiting on my arrival since plans had already been made and the appointment set and they would perform abortions up to your 6th month, my family had planned that I would move back home, start school in the Fall, and life would carry on. Well, that was NOT my idea at all! I would NOT kill my baby, period end of subject!

A few weeks pass, and I had begun gathering things that I would need for my new arrival on November 19, 1980. I had decided that his name would be "Johnathan DeWayne", I found a beautiful hand-made bassinet at a garage sale, began buying newborn diapers, and newborn clothes. My family comes over to my apartment one day and announces that since I would not have an abortion, they had decided that giving the baby up for adoption would be the next best thing and they had already made an appointment with the Edna Gladney Center for pregnant girls for a first meeting and interview. Again, Not my idea, and NOT what I was willing to do until the ultimatum came. Since it was obvious that I wasn't going along with any plans made for my life the ultimatum was given, either give up the baby for adoption or give up ALL of my family, and never have any contact with ANYONE from my family ever again, period, end of subject! Now, here I was, single, pregnant, working full-time at a good job, and being force to make the biggest decision of my life. Choosing between my baby and my family connections, what was an 18 year old going to do?

A few more weeks went by, and my decision had to be made, since I was beginning to show very well by this time, and my family didn't want me coming around anymore being unmarried and "big as a barrel". I cried a lot thinking of what life was going to be like without any family members, grandparents, aunts, uncles, cousins, etc.… and the gut wrenching choice to lose my first born child and NEVER to see him again so began the consideration of the option placed in front of me. Naturally, as an 18 year old, only child, I didn't want to lose my family forever, so I reluctantly agreed to their plans on me giving up my baby. They moved me home for a couple of days and I wasn't allowed to be seen outside the house, for fear of what the neighbors might think, until they could get us all moved into an apartment in another town, so I could continue to work at my job, up until my due date and not be seen by the neighbors. Plans were made that I would move into the Edna Gladney Center a few days prior to my due date just prior to Thanksgiving in November, so I wouldn't have to take that much time off from work.

Thanksgiving Day 1980 came, and since I was still in the Center and still hadn't given birth yet, my parents, decided that we would go out around town car shopping. See, since they hadn't given my anything as a graduation gift, they decided that when I got out of the Edna Gladney Center, they would make the down payment on a new car for me. I believe this was a way of paying me off for what I was about to do.

Finally, December 11, 1980 at 5 a.m., labor begins! I make the phone call to my parents telling them that I am at the hospital on the campus, and fixing to "cross over". That's what the Center called it when any of us girls would go into labor and, we didn't call it labor and delivery, we called it, crossing over or going over. I guess it made it somehow easier to deal with than actually saying that you were in labor and fixing to deliver a baby that you would never see again. Labor was INTENSE, and it was back labor on top of that, which I am told is more painful. A few hours into crossing over, and "Johnathan" was in trouble. At 10:45 a.m., they slap an oxygen mask on me, and tell me to "BREATHE DEEP" because my baby was dying! They rush me into the operating room and performed an emergency C-Section. The nurses told me later that when "Johnathan" was born, he farted and his water sack was filled with fecal material, because for the entire 10-months of pregnancy, his head had been outside the water sack, and basically he had been breathing air for the last portion of the pregnancy, which caused him to have air (gas) in his system. They called him an "over cooked" baby, and that the fetal distress was caused by the fact that he was a 10-month baby, had been outside of the water sack for the length of my pregnancy, my cervix was not dilating as it should, and there was no way that my pelvis was wide enough for me to deliver a 4 pound baby, let alone a 6 or 7 pound baby, which is where he started out at. "Johnathan" weighed in at 5 pounds 10 ounces, and 22 inches long when he was born. The continuation of Johnathan's Touch will be in another chapter; however, you needed the background story for the full impact of what this birth mother did and learned through the process of this unexpected arrival.

#2 Points To Ponder

Unexpected arrivals are simply unexpected blessings waiting for us to make the right decisions connected to them. Most of the time when we have unexpected suddenlies happen in our lives, they are a time of decision for us, and based on the decisions that we make will determine the blessings that will come from them. In the previous stories, we find that everyone's reactions and decisions made had a direct bearing on the blessings that followed those decisions. Throughout the Bible and Life, we find this to be true as well.

In life, have you ever wondered why when some people have an unexpected win fall of money like winning the lottery, statics show that within five years some of those same people are in worse shape than they were prior to the unexpected win fall. The reason is simple they failed to make the correct decisions surrounding their unexpected arrival and it in essence their unexpected arrival became a curse to them. It's not because money is evil, or even that the lottery is evil, it is simply the choices that some people make when faced with an unexpected arrival choose wrongly. The same thing could have happened to anyone of the people connected to the stories that we just read. Their decisions, had they made them differently could have become curses on their lives and that lives around them.

The Bible put these choices even clearer in the following scriptures; Deuteronomy 11:26–28 – "Behold, I set before you today a blessing and a curse: the blessing if you obey the commandment of the LORD you God which I command you today; and the curse, if you do not obey the commandment of the LORD your God but run aside from the way which I command you today, to go after other gods which you have not known." Deuteronomy 30:19–20 – "I call heaven and earth as witnesses today against you, that I have set before you, life and death, blessing and cursing; therefore choose life, that both you and your descendants may live; that you may love the LORD your God, that you may obey His voice, and that you may cling to Him, for he is your life and the length of your days; and that you may dwell in the land which the LORD swore to your fathers, to Abraham, Issac, and Jacob, to give them." God has a way of love, life and obedience, and the opposite of God's way is a way of hate, death and disobedience, the choice is yours to make, Blessing or Curse. HINT: Choose LIFE and Blessing!

I am reminded of the story in Luke chapter 1 of the unexpected arrival of John the Baptist, and how, when Zacharias, his father was told that his wife would become pregnant with a child even though they were advanced in age. Zacharias questioned the Angel Gabriel, and because his question wasn't in faith believing that this was true, the angel proclaimed that he would be mute until the day of John the Baptist's birth. And so it was that Zacharias was mute until the day that John was born. I truly believe that because Zacharias' question was not in faith believing at the time he was given this information, had the angel not shut Zacharias' mouth, that this man could have created such controversy surrounding the Birth of John the Baptist, that it could have impacted what John was called to do from birth and that was to be the forerunner to Jesus' entrance. Moreover, notice the differences between Zacharias' question and the question that Mary asked. Luke 1:34 – Then Mary said to the angel, "How can this be, since I do not know a man.?" Luke 1:18 – And Zacharias said to the angel, "How shall I know this? For I am an old man and my wife is well advance in years." Notice Mary accepted what the angel had said as being true, while Zacharias question how he would know this is true. See the difference in faith verses disbelief?

Some of the decisions that these people made had a direct impact on everyone in the world, and others only impacted those surrounding the unexpected arrival, and then impacted the lives of you who are reading their stories. Either way, you will be impacted by the choices and decisions that others have made, and I pray that they will cause you to think differently when you experience an unexpected arrival in your life. The following section further expounds on these choices that we sometimes must make throughout our lives, and how those choices impact others around us as well.

SECTION III

Adoption Into A New Life

Galatians 4: 4–7

However, when the fullness of the time had come, God sent forth His Son, born of a woman, born under the law, to redeem those who were under the law, that we might receive the adoption as sons.

And because you are sons, God has sent forth the Spirit of His Son into your hearts, crying out. "Abba, Father!" Therefore you are no longer a slave but a son, and if a son, then an heir of God through Christ.

8

Johnathan's Touch – Part Two
Birth Mother Prays To An Unknown God

WE LEFT PART one of Johnathan's Touch in chapter 7 at Johnathan's dramatic arrival into the world, at 5 pounds 10 ounces and 22 inches long. In a typical case where the birth mother is giving up her rights to her newborn child, the agency wants this part of the transaction completed as quickly as possible. However, there were complications, and I was running a very high fever for 7 days after Johnathan's birth. I demanded that I would not sign any paper work until I was able to see him just one time before signing the papers. Now mind you, the agency doesn't like the birth mother to see the child, because often times the birth mother once they see their child, will decide NOT to give up their child and simply walk out of the hospital with child in hand. Such was not the case or an option in my situation because if I had walked out of the hospital, I knew what I would be walking out on in other regards, my entire family connection, and as an 18 year old girl, couldn't comprehend that not having any family connection might have been a good thing.

For the entire seven days that I spent in the hospital sick because of the infection coursing through my body, I had only one visitor every other evening. Finally, the day came that my fever broke somewhat down to 99 from what it had been consistently running 103 to 104 for the past 7 days, and I was allowed to see Johnathan for a few minutes. They led me into this small closet type room with a short hard bench type thing for me to sit on. As I sat there waiting for them to bring Johnathan in, I had NO emotion regarding the situation, it almost seemed like a dream or something. Moments later, a nurse brought him in and handed him to me in this tight little bundle, and then turned and walked out of the room. I sat there, holding him with my arms almost out stretched so I could take him all in as fast as I could. He had the deepest blue eyes, and a full head of coal black hair; he was already in need of a haircut actually. I was told that I had exactly 10 minutes and the nurse would be back to take him back to the nursery, so I was going to make the most of the few minutes that I had.

As Johnathan and I sat there staring at one another, I began to cry almost sobbing, and began praying to a God that I did not know, that He was in charge of making sure that my baby had a good and loving home to go home to, with parents that would always be fair and treat him with the special care that he deserved. I explained to God, that I could not give him a family that would give him the type of special care and attention he deserved. I further explained to this unknown God that Johnathan was a special boy, and needed a special family that would always love and protect him no matter what he might do to disappoint them, and that his new family would NEVER give him the ultimatums that I was facing or have to make the choices that I was having to make. At that very moment, the room seemed to become brighter with some unnaturally bright light, and as I looked down at Johnathan's face, I thought for a moment that I almost saw him smile as he reached out his little hand and grabbed hold of my little finger. With Johnathan's touch, somehow I knew that I had just rounded the corner into a new life, along with giving him a new family. Little did I realize then what this new life was all about, or even how I ended up on the journey that I was about to embark. Just then, the door flew open, another nurse rushed in and took Johnathan out of my arms, and another woman ushered me into the visitor's waiting room of the hospital. There this dark haired lady began to hand me all this paper work and told me that I needed to sign each and every document now that I had seen my baby, and that as soon as the papers were signed I would be released from the hospital, allowed to go home, and then Johnathan's new parents could come and pick him up as well. She told me that they had been waiting in a local hotel waiting for her to call them to come pick him up, but that they couldn't release him until I was out of the center, so as to protect the privacy of the new parents.

As I sat there in my dazed state listening to everything that she said about the papers that I was signing, and somehow not really hearing anything that she said, as I signed the last piece of paper, I began to cry, and marveled at how with a couple of signatures a life could be signed away. As soon as I finished signing the final paper, she rushed them out of my hand, stood up, and walked out of the room, leaving me to my bewildered state. Then I returned to my room, gathered my things, and left the hospital through the front door and never looked back, until I went back on Johnathan's 18th birthday on December 11, 1998, so that if or when he came looking for me, there would be a current address in their files.

As my family had come to the hospital to take me home that day, and the only thing that was said as we were pulling out of the parking lot was well that's over now we can go on with our lives. I had no response, no emotion, simply numbness that seemed to envelope my entire body, I don't even remember if I even had any thoughts running through my head as we drove down the freeways, and oddly enough, I have never been able to remember the rest of that car ride. When we arrived home, I walked in and the thing that struck me first is I felt like a stranger in the only house that I was ever raised in. It was no longer a homey feeling, but a feeling that I was a guest, an unwelcome guest at that, in a place I used to call home.

The next morning I woke up, and found my way slowly to the living room turned on the TV and there was a church service on and they were announcing the new births and arrivals of babies into some of the families that went to that church. It struck me that in some of the announcements they would say a particular family had a new birth and in one of the announcements, they announced that a family was announcing the new arrival of their son, Princeton into their family. As I pondered what I had just heard on that church program, I wondered and wondered for years after that day if that wasn't somehow my little Johnathan that was being welcomed into his new life and family, and somehow I got to hear that announcement that day.

THE UNWRITTEN LETTER

Dearest Johnathan,

I realized that this letter is many years late, but honestly, I didn't know what to write to you when you were first born. Not that I really know what to write now, except I can only hope that your family whom chose you to be their son, was the best family ever for and to you and you had the childhood to be proud of. By a complete surprise to me a search angel contacted me and told me that you had been located. When I first saw your picture that was an answer to many years of praying that one day, I would be able to see your face. I always knew that we would see each other in Heaven, but my prayer was that I could see your grownup face THIS SIDE of HEAVEN, and that wonderful search angel helped in answering that prayer request. It was a special added benefit that I was able to see pictures of your children as well.

    I hope that one day I will be able to see you and your family, and hug each one of you, if only for a moment. I know that you have a mother whom you love very much, however I would like to have at least a friendship with you and your family. I NEVER forgot you; I NEVER stopped loving you and your younger brothers and sisters were always told that one day I was expecting that you would show up at our door. I believe I have said the rest of what I wanted to say to you in the previous two chapters about you. Now if you have any questions please don't hesitate to contact me at the contact information that I have provided you.

Many Blessings and MUCH LOVE,
Your Birth Mother – Cammy Walters

9

Donald The Destined Son

As a 3-year-old adopted daughter of the Most High God, 29 years old in biological age, little did I know just how much he truly loves and cares for every aspect of his children's lives, however, I was soon to find out. Allow me to back up for just a bit. Remember I have already shared with you Johnathan's Touch, and how that I had given Johnathan up for adoption at birth. Now I was going to learn that my heavenly Father God never forgot that prayer that I prayed that day over Johnathan, now my daddy God was going to give me another son.

Being a single mother of two children, and recently divorced for the second time in my life, had NO INTENTIONS of ever getting married again. I still wanted to go out on dates, but never more than twice with the same person, simply because I felt that if I dated anyone more than twice, that meant that we were getting to know one another, and THAT WASN'T HAPPENING AGAIN! I had run a personal ad in our local newspaper titled: "Lady loves everything…long walks, a good laugh, and simple times etc…" just looking for someone to go out to see a movie and have dinner with, and I started a list of men that responded. As I generated this list of men that had called and left their name and message to me, as I got to number 10 on the list, this one bothered me. This man's message didn't bother me in a bad sense, but I had this overwhelming fear…."Oh, no…I am not calling that guy back, because I will get married to that one, and that is OUT OF THE QUESTION". So as the days rolled by, and the messages kept adding up on my list, I kept having this knowing feeling that I needed to respond to this number 10 guy, so I called and we talked a little while, however we still didn't set a first date to meet yet.

During the conversation, I still had an unnerving feeling that if I met this man in person that we would somehow become serious and become married in no time. I discussed this man with my best girlfriend, and during our conversation, we decided that I would go and meet him; however, she wanted all his facts before I left, just in case something bad happened to me so she would have a place to start looking, and a way to find this person. Therefore, I went home that evening from her house and decided that I would call him to see if we could just go out for coffee sometime and that would be the end of it so I thought. I was just trying to get this nagging feeling to go away that I needed to meet number 10. Much to my surprise, this man was eagerly awaiting my call, and said, "Yes, how about now?" Now here it is 8 or 9 o'clock at night, and probably one of the darkest nights I had ever seen before, and we are both rushing around to get to a Denney's restaurant in Irving, Texas to meet each other for the first time. Little did I know then that I was walking straight into my destined child's life, in the destiny that my Father God had already prepared for me to walk into.

I arrived at the restaurant, and for some reason it was packed....the parking lot was so full that I had to drive around the building twice just to try to find a parking place. On the second time around the building, I passed this Old Red Chevy Nova, and as I saw the driver, I just knew that he was the man that I was to meet, and now terror struck me again..."Oh no, this is the man that I am fixing to get married to?" As I parked the car, and really wanted to just drive back home, something compelled me to go in and talk with this man. We introduced ourselves to each other, and were seated. From the first minute that we laid eyes on each other, we knew that this was somehow all going to work out...not exactly sure how, but that it was meant to be somehow. As we sat and talked the hours rolled by...1, 2, 3, 4 hours later, and we had discussed everything from how to raise kids, to what each of us was looking for in a prospective life partner, to what happens when the children are grown and fly away from the nest. Literally, that night was our Holy Spirit guided pre-marriage counseling session, and a meeting that was soon to change our lives and the lives of our combined five children forever.

Now, this wasn't the time that I had wanted to happen, but it was the destiny that God had designed for each of us. As my husband and I went out on our first official date, he was such a gentleman, and we thoroughly enjoyed our time out together. We took thing very slowly in the beginning, and it was about a month after we had started dating that we would finally meet each other's children. We made plans that I would bring my 2 year old son and 8 year old daughter to his house and we would take all the kids to the park for hamburgers and hotdogs that Saturday afternoon. The kids and I arrived as expected at his house, and his 6 year old son and 13 and 14 year old daughters were playing with the neighborhood girls next door. As I was sitting on the sofa facing the front door of his house, his kids appeared at the door. As the door opened his son stepped in first and what a sight... Here this little boy is, the only boy in the neighborhood, standing and meeting me for the first time, after having been dressed up by his sisters the and neighborhood girls. His hair was in curlers with a big floppy hat on top, makeup all over his face, a dress that looked like the neighbor's mom had given them, and high-heeled shoes....this was quite a sight to behold. All of the sudden, I hear, like someone whispering in my right ear, "This is your Son"....I chuckled and said within myself... "Yes, it probably is". Now, no one was standing whispering in my ear literally, and what I would learn later is that this is the way that the Holy Spirit of God would talk with me throughout my life as a child of the Most High, in a still small voice, in my right ear.

Now, I didn't understand what was said to me that day since Donald had a biological mother she was just in jail at the time, and really, I had dismissed the fact that Don and I were destined to get married. I just thought the statement was strange, and just didn't understand it completely. Therefore, with everything that I don't understand, I simply placed it on a shelf within my mind until understanding comes. I didn't tell anyone that day what I heard, because I just don't repeat things that I don't understand. We simply continued building the relationship between ourselves and all the kids, and we got married exactly one year to the day that we met at that Denney's restaurant, and is why when any one ever asks how long we have been married, we have two numbers instead of just one, such as at the time of this writing we have been married 19-20.

Now, every blended family knows that there are going to be difficulties merging the families especially when you have 5 children involved, and ex-spouses. However, the problems multiply when one of the ex-spouses dies, which is what happened to Donald's biological mother when he was only 7 years old, and 11 months into Don's and my marriage. The day after Donald's biological mother died, I called the school counselor to let her know what had just happened in our family and asked if she would please keep an eye on Donald to make sure that he was ok, and to let us know if he started showing any signs of grief or depression that we might need to know about.

One afternoon a few weeks after her death, the school counselor called to talk to us and shared with us that Donald was doing fine, after she finally determined that he wasn't having delusions of his mother. The school counselor would talk with Donald everyday just to check up on him and ask how home life was, and he would tell her about what him and his Mom and Dad did that weekend, or evening. The Counselor was confused until one day she finally understood that Mom was me, and that he was referring to me and his dad and what the family was doing. Therefore, when the counselor determined that Donald was adjusting quite well, and her concerns were alleviated, she called to inform us that the only Mom that he considered Mom was me, and that he was a very well adjusted little boy for the traumatic experience that had just gone in the family. She even made the statement to me during our conversation; "God placed Donald in your life at just the right time".

Time went on and our family suffering from a few war wounds of merging families with teenage daughters, two of which had lost their biological mother. We decided that we needed to move to the country to get away from the city problems and issues; the gangs and cults that seemed to be assailing our family. When Don brought up the idea of moving to a small rural community, my first reaction was "Yes, the gangs and cult have gotten hold of our girls, and they are NOT going to get our boys! So off we began to look for our home in the country. Now we were not rich people, and we were still raising our children and living paycheck to paycheck barely making ends meet each month. Many times, there would be more month left than money, but we made it with God Grace, and didn't know exactly how we were going to be able to purchase a home in the country.

Now, I was in the mortgage business, so I knew that there were a few things that we could possibly do to get into a house, one of which was find an assumable loan, which would be the cheapest way to get into one. Every day, Don would bring home the newspaper from work and show me what he had found on his lunch break. Every evening we would call on the houses that he had found, and so the process would continue. One day some friends of our had 10 acres of land just outside of Springtown, Texas that they wanted to sell, and we grabbed it as soon as they asked if we wanted it. Now, we had land, all we needed to do now is to find a house to rent that we could afford, and start building a house on that property. At that time Springtown was a rural community, just beginning to have a growth spurt of city people wanting to move to the country. Property values and rents were on the rise, and Don and I didn't know how we were ever going to rent a place, make the monthly land payments and build a house at the same time, and all on his 13 dollars per hour that he was making at his job, and my sporadic income as a loan officer at a mortgage company. Armed with "They aren't going to get our boys!" we began to make plans that if we had to we would live in a tent on the property and build our house. God had other plans!

Remember all the phone calls that we had made prior to purchasing our land, well one of those people that we had called, called us back and said that they didn't know what had happened to the person that was supposed to buy their house, but that buyer just seemed to disappear off the face of the earth, and they couldn't find him any longer, and said, "If you are still interested in the house it's yours if you want it". Elated over the news of a real house and not a tent, Don sent the boys and me out to look at it the next morning, and if I liked it, we would buy it. The boys were thrilled, and asked if they could have a dog when we moved in, and were excited to see that it already had a basketball goal just waiting for them. I was excited, because not only was I not going to have to live in a tent, but that this house just happen to be a house that I had dreams of as a little girl, Red wagon wheels, horseshoe drive and all. God kept us out of a tent!!!!

Moving day arrived, and we made sure that one of the first things that we brought were the boys bikes so that they could keep busy playing while we unloaded the first load. Well, as city kids, they didn't have the understanding of how differently rock driveways and concrete driveways were until CRASH…Donald had his first wipeout, and learned that gravel and rocks move underneath narrow bike tires. Limping and bleeding he comes into the house and we soon learn that we had forgotten the first aid kit back in Irving. So I clean him up the best I could, and off he went again, to play in his new HUGE yard with lots of trees to climb and places to explore, armed with his new knowledge that gravel and rocks move.

The first week in our new home, the boys were excitedly waiting for their new dogs that we had told them that they could have as soon as we got move in. I found a person not far from us that had just had a litter of puppies, and the boys and I go to see them. Donald was the first one to find the one he wanted, it was a brown haired little girl puppy, and he named her Katie. Marcus found his puppy and he named her Lassie, and so the story continues about boys and their dogs, mom, being the kind soul that I am, didn't want to leave the other puppy by himself, so I even got a puppy that day! So we were off to the grocery store to get the puppy chow, and toys. Katie and Donald were the best of friends, and I know that it sounds strange but they even seemed to resemble one another with their sandy blonde hair color and bright brown-eyed looks.

Donald is such a great kid, with a smile that seemed to just melt your heart, and he knew how to work that big bright smile to his advantage every time. In school, Donald was the class clown, and I would tell all of his teachers, don't let him get away with anything, because once you do, you have lost his attention and respect for the rest of the year. Donald was our child that liked a very structured lifestyle, and wanted to always know that you were there for him and weren't going anywhere but that you meant what you said, and said what you meant. If you ever told Donald that there was a consequence to his actions, and didn't follow through with what you said, you lost his attention and his respect for your authority. Somehow, we could never make any of his teachers understand this concept with the exception of one, his fourth grade teacher, Mrs. Hampton. Once she learned this, she was the only teacher that Donald ever truly admired and respected even after all these years he still talks about how great she was.

When Donald was 10 years old, Don and I learned that in the state of Texas where we live, if something were to happen to a biological parent of a child, the state could and would step in and remove the child from the stepparent and place that child with biological family members. Regardless of what we had written in our wills, our boys would be ripped away from each other, and the surviving parent, and sent off to live with family that didn't know them or want them. Therefore, our attorney advised us, that to protect our boys we needed to file to adopt each other's children, and thus avoid any problems should something happen to one of us. Now, don't miss-understand me, Don and I never felt like we were stepparents, and neither did we ever treat each other's children like stepparents. We would continually receive comments from people and friends that it was hard for them to figure out whose children were whose, because we treated them all equally, and had the same authority with all of them. I guess it was just the supernatural God intervention within our family that caused this situation. Therefore, when Donald was 10 years old we started the process of adopting each other's boys. Donald was 11 years old and his time for adoption came, and I was never more proud and honored to hear him answer the Judge when he asked, "Who do you want to be your Mother to be?", and Donald smiled that Big Wide Smile of his and told the Judge, well, my Mom of course as he pointed at me. Such an honored moment, and one you only get with adopted children that are old enough in the courts eyes, to be able to make a choice and decision for themselves. As we were standing having our picture taken with the Judge that day, I heard in my right ear again, "See, This is your Son".

10

Tori's Arrival

FOR ANYONE WHO has ever adopted a child, you know that often times it doesn't go as smoothly as we expect, or without a certain amount of drama surrounding the drama. Such was the case with Tori's arrival. And for those of you that have never adopted a child, don't think for a minute that the adoptive parents don't have some type to drama surrounding the fact that they are trying to do a "Good Thing" and that they aren't going to have to go through hell to get there. Joann and Ferris having just come out of a situation with their previous child that was stillborn because of a critical birth defect make the decision, or I should say Joann makes the decision that she wasn't going out on a bad note with having children after the birth of their last child. You will read about Tobi in an upcoming chapter, for now, Joann is determined that she will not stop having children just because they had to release Tobi to Heaven.

Joann and Ferris are ministers at their church, and Joann being the caring and compassionate person that she is knew of a couple that desperately wanted a baby, and Joann was in constant prayer for this couple. One day Joann arrives at church, and Sarah a friend of hers walks up to her that begins telling her about this teenage girl who is pregnant and the parents and the teenager want to give the baby up for adoption, in the best interest for the child. See, the family knows that if it were to remain within the family, that baby would be tossed around, and not have a very good life because of some of the situations involved. Joann, immediately said, "I know exactly the parents for this baby, and this would be a perfect adoption, with no problems." Joann believed that this baby was the answer to her prayers for the couple that wanted a child. Joann being now pregnant with her own child, and having lots of other children knew how important it is for a woman who is having trouble conceiving their own child would love, and care for any child that was place in their home. Joann knew that this was the answer for them.

After church that Sabbath day on the drive home, as Joann is telling Ferris that she had found a baby for the couple that was wanting a baby, he spoke up and said, "Joann, if you want to adopt that baby, we can do that", and her response was "NO, that's their baby that I have been praying for them about." When Joann and Ferris arrived home she immediately called this woman, and she was so excited to tell her that she had a baby for them. Joann just knew that the couple would rush over and they all would be singing, dancing, and praising Yahweh, for bringing them the baby that they so desired. After hanging up the phone, Joann was a little disappointed that the response was not what she had thought it should have been, but soon dismissed the disappointment knowing that this family might have wanted to celebrate with their own family and announce that they had a baby on the way. As the hours passed and turned into days, Joann began having a sick feeling that somehow this couple didn't want this baby. Finally, the call came, but it wasn't exactly what Joann had expected. The woman begins asking for further information about the baby, and Joann had some of the answers but not all of them at the time. Joann tells her, let me find out, and I'll call you right back. Joann calls Sarah and asks for the additional information, and gathers everything that she believed that the woman was asking for. An hour later she calls the woman back and tells her that the nationality of the baby would be part Hispanic, which Joann didn't see a real issue, but it was what the couple wanted to know. The woman tells Joann, well, ok, let me tell my husband what you have found out and I'll call you back. Hours turned into days again, finally the call comes, and again, not what Joann was expecting. The woman on the other end of the phone says, "Joann, there is no way that he will adopt a Hispanic child, I am sorry, but he just won't do that." Now, Joann shocked by the response that she was just given, about an answer to prayer for this family, hung up the phone. Joann said, "I had no sooner hung up the phone until I was picking it up again trying to find a lawyer, because Daddy had already said that we could adopt this baby!"

So now, the stage of Joann and Ferris' life as adoptive parents is set so let the chaos begin! Now, what you don't know about Joann and Ferris is that they are currently pregnant with another child of their own, and now they are going to be adopting this child. Tori, their adopted child will be their 12th child, and Morgan in Joann's womb is to be child number 11, according to the due dates of each of the children. Joann is so excited because the children are to be born only a few weeks apart and she said "that it would be like we have a set of twins, and she hadn't had any twins yet, and this would be fun."

Plans had already been made that Joann would film the birth of her sister's child since it was being born by C-Section in just a few weeks and would be an anencephalic baby like her previous child had been. Joann not realizing how traumatic this event would be for her, and not realizing the emotional impact that it would have on her, was shocked at how this birth affected her, but she handled it with all the grace and style of the classy woman of Yahweh that she is. Her sister and brother-in-law had several other children at home, and Joann went home with the family to help out for a few days after their baby was born. Their anencephalic baby lived for 7 months after birth, and needed round the clock care. Joann made the decision that she needed to go home to be with her children, and took her sister's 4 youngest children home with her as well. Now here Joann is with 8 children at home already, takes 4 more home, she is pregnant with number 11 and adopting number 12 soon. Not what you would consider a stress free environment, or one that you would expect to have going on, but this is their life right now.

A few days after having all the children at home with her, each one begins coming down with strange illnesses, one has seemed to have lost the ability to walk, one has had an accident and hit his head on the hearth and has gone temporarily blind from the hit on the head, and suddenly, one begins having Grand Mal seizures for no reason and is in the hospital for 5 days. Finally, 4 of the children go back home to their mom and dad, and Joann and Ferris have now been able to bring their child home from the hospital late one evening, when the phone rings in the middle of the night. It's the family of the mother that is giving them her baby, telling them that they know that it's 6 to 8 weeks early, but the baby is being born at any time now.

Joann now running on empty emotionally, still pregnant with what is now going to be baby number 12 instead of baby number 11, and now she is having to pack everyone up to go to the hospital for Tori's arrival. Joann said, "I was moving in slow motion it seemed and finally I had gotten everything gathered for everyone to go to the hospital." Oh, and the best part, in all the chaos, Joann and Ferris had forgotten to tell the family members that they were adopting a baby, so the children didn't find out until they are on the way to the hospital that they had a baby sister now. Joann and Ferris had planned that they would be telling the children the following weekend after everything calmed down a bit, and we see how well that worked out for them.

Arriving at the hospital, Joann knowing that Tori was very premature, and knowing sort of what to expect, opened the door to the nursery, and saw tubes coming out of every orifice of her little body, said..."Wow, she looks so good, this is a whole baby, and she looks so good, this is something that I can work with her, she looks good." The nurses not understand what Joann had already been through with her previous child, thought that she was a little off in her thinking that this little 4 pound 5 ounce premature baby looks good to her remarked, "She looks good?" Joann said, "She look GREAT, she looks great to me she has a head and this is a whole baby!"

Adopting a newborn baby straight from the hospital was an experience that Joann had never been versed in and soon learned the legal issues surrounding such an adoption. See, when a new born baby is placed for adoption in the hospital, the birth parents will sign their parental rights away, but the adoptive parents are not considered the legal parents until the birth mother leaves the hospital, so the baby is actually in "legal limbo" until the birth mother leaves the hospital. So this causes a few issues for Joann ability to stay with the baby, until the birth mother walks out of the hospital doors. Once the birth mother leaves, the law now sees the adoptive parents as the legal parents, with full parental rights and privileges.

Within two weeks, Joann and Ferris are able to take their new adopted baby girl home, and so begins their new life as adoptive parents. Joann's pregnancy goes 3 weeks past her due date and she believe that this was another gift from Yahweh, to allow her time with Tori that Tori really needed as a premature baby. With premature babies, they have been so over stimulated by all the poking and attention, and bright lights of the nursery and hospital, that often times, it is too much for them to take in and they simply withdraw inside themselves as a protective measure. They many times, will not look you in the eye, smile or sometimes will not respond to any attention. Joann said that it took about 2 months before Tori would begin to look them in the eye instead of looking past them, and began to respond with any affection shown, and Joann said, "Mission accomplished!" Joann said that being Tori was 2-1/2 months older than Morgan, allowed the cuddle time and attention that Tori needed and might not have received if they had been born according to their due dates.

Joann said "that the extended family was supportive they maybe thought we were a little weird, but supportive of our decision and actually Ferris dad had paid the $5,000 that it cost for Tori's adoption as his special little gift. She said the only problem that they had was about two or three weeks had pasted since we brought Tori home, and their 7 year old seemed to have an attitude toward them, not the baby, but toward them. He was just mad, mad at them, and they didn't understand why." One day Joann asked him what the problem was and he said, "I can't believe you took that woman's baby away from her, how could you do that?" Somehow, he had missed the part that they were adopting Tori, and that the mother had given Tori to them.

The most fun that Joann and Ferris have is when they are out and about in town and the people always say how much Tori looks like her dad, she said, "We just smile and laugh to ourselves and thank them." She continued by saying, "The thing is Yahweh always guides you and that is what I have learned through all of my life experiences. I now have the confidence that I don't care what I have to go through, I can go through it, I don't care how bad it is, I don't care how rough it might be, Yahweh will take me through it and there will come the day when I'll smile again, and all will be well. You might not see Yahweh's hand as you are going through whatever it is, but I promise you when you get through it and you look back, you will see Yahweh's hand every step of the way." The sign that hangs in the front entry of Joann and Ferris home says, "We may not have it all together, but together we have it all" which sums up this awesome family.

#3 Points To Ponder

THE INTERESTING FACT about adoption is that it isn't a man-developed idea, but a God ordained plan. The plan of adoption began before the fall of man; when God created Man and sinful man fell, God's plan "A" was always Adoption! God wanted a family, so He GAVE his only begotten son, so that whosoever should believe in Him would be ADOPTED into the family. Notice if you will that God was the first biological parent that GAVE His son, and also, God was the first Adoptive parent to adopt more children into His family. For you who may be unaware of this Adoption I want to discuss a list of scriptures that clearly show this to be true. For those of you that understand your adoption into God's family, these scriptures will only help to solidify your understanding.

In the following paragraph, I took my liberty with the scripture to bring my point across about God's adoption plan. The actual scripture reads: John 3:16 – For God so loved the world that He gave his only begotten Son, that whoever believes in Him should not perish but have everlasting life. One fact that most people don't understand about adoption in the United States today, is that in our state of Texas, and I am sure in several other states, an adoptive parent signs and swears an oath that they will never and can never disown their child that have received into their family through the adoption procedures. They could and some parents have disowned their natural children, however they can NEVER disown their adoptive children, it is simply legally not allowed. This is also true for anyone that believes in God's only begotten Son and becomes an Adopted member into the family of God, it is forever, and the adoptee can never be disowned from the family.

John 1:12–13 – tells us that "But as many as received Him, to them He gave the right to become children of God, to those who believe in His name: who were born, not of blood, nor of the will of the flesh, nor of the will of man, but of God." Notice it wasn't man's idea but actually by God's own will that if you believe in God's only begotten Son, Jesus, that you have the same rights to become children of God, which makes Jesus your elder brother, simply by believing that Jesus is God's only begotten Son. Very simple, very easy, and just like a child that is adopted into a family here on earth. The child doesn't have to do anything except believe that these parents are their new parents and their siblings are indeed their siblings. No work, no struggle, just fact, and the simple act of believing on the child's part. Paperwork and legal red tape on the parent's part and the extreme cost of His Son's red blood on God's part.

To further cement the fact that adoption was always God's plan "A", we will now look at Romans 8:14–17 – "For as many as are led by the Spirit of God, these are sons of God. For you did not receive the spirit of bondage again to fear but you received the Spirit of Adoption by whom we cry out, 'Abba Father.' The Spirit Himself bears witness with our spirit that we are children of God and if children then heirs – heirs of God and joint heirs with Christ, if indeed we suffer with Him, that we may also be glorified together."

Orphans and children in need of new parents all experience the same struggle and that struggle is with fear, and that is the reason that God put in His word, that as sons you have not received the bondage again of fear. Children are always afraid when there is not a parental covering, and God wants to give us no doubt that fear is no longer an issue now that we can cry out "Abba Father".

Ephesians 1:3–14 – "Blessed be the God and Father of our Lord Jesus Christ, who has blessed us with every spiritual blessing in the heavenly places in Christ, just as He chose us in Him before the foundation of the world, that we should be holy and without blame before Him in love, having predestined us to adoption as sons by Jesus Christ to Himself, according to the good pleasure of His will, to the praise of the glory of His grace, by which He made us accepted in the Beloved.

In Him we have redemption through His blood, the forgiveness of sins, according to the riches of His grace which He made to abound toward us in all wisdom and prudence having made known to us the mystery of His will, according to His good pleasure which He purposed in Himself, that in the dispensation of the fullness of the times He might gather together in one all things in Christ, both which are in heaven and which are on earth – in Him. In Him, also we have obtained an inheritance, being predestined according to the purpose of Him who works all things according to the counsel of His will that we who first trusted in Christ should be to the praise of His glory.

In Him you also trusted, after you heard the word of truth, the gospel of your salvation; in whom also, having believed, you were sealed with the Holy Spirit of promise, who is the guarantee of our inheritance until the redemption of the purchase possession, to the praise of His glory."

After showing God's plan "A" has always been Adoption, I pray that you have or will accept the Son, and become a joint heir of God, with me and Jesus and we will all be rejoicing in Heaven throughout eternity. It doesn't matter what you have done or been in your life only that you believe on Him as God's only begotten Son. I promise all the red tape has already been done, all you must do is to believe. Regardless of whether or not you have experienced what we will be talking about in the next section, you are accepted in the Beloved if you only believe on God's only begotten Son there is No Condemnation to those who are in Christ Jesus, and heirs according to God's promise.

Section IV

An Aborted Life

Micah 7:18–19

Who is a God like you, Pardoning iniquity and passing over the transgression of the remnant of His heritage? He does not retain His anger forever, Because He delights in mercy. He will again have compassion on us, And will subdue our iniquities. You will cast all our sins into the depths of the sea.

Matthew 7:1–5

"Judge not, that you be not judged. For with what judgment you judge, you will be judged; and with the measure you use, it will be measured back to you. And why do you look at the speck in your brother's eye, but do not consider the plank in your own eye? Or how can you say to your brother, 'Let me remove the speck from your eye'; and look, a plank is in your own eye. Hypocrite! First remove the plank from your own eye, and then you will see clearly to remove the speck from your brother's eye."

11

Shawna's Soul Tie

As the mother of 7 children, and grandmother of 16 grandchildren, I felt I needed to include this chapter into the book for the hope and healing of parents and grandparents out there. Hope to grandparents, especially grandmothers that are grieving the loss of a grandchild, and healing to parents that have chosen to abort a child because they felt that there was no other option. We all have and make choices throughout our life, and we need to remember that those choices whether good or bad have consequences, not only to ourselves but also to others that are connected to our lives. Regardless of whether you are a step grandparent, biological grandparent, stepparent, or biological parent within a family unit, the emotional ties that bind are still there, are very real, and God given ties that connect us to one another, the term for this is Soul Ties.

Soul ties are like the umbilical cord within the womb that attaches the baby to the mothers' life support system. These cords connect our life to others within a family unit and other relationships that we may have, and are supposed to supply the necessary nutrition that the every member needs as well as a means of carrying off the waste that is created and needs to be expelled in order for healthy relationships to flourish and thrive. Soul ties can also be a toxic tie within family and relationship dynamics that aren't healthy to begin with and are carrying waste products each direction, there by contaminating all parties involved in a toxic way. For the purposes of this chapter, we will only be dealing with healthy soul tie connections and their importance in healing when there has been an abortion or death of a child within the family unit and how those ties connect us to the death of that child.

Parents that have lost a child to death, whether by choice, accident, disease or illness, believe that their pain is only their pain, and that it isn't the same for the other members of the extended family. This is a completely wrong assumption on the part of the parent because of the Soul Ties that God has attached to each family member within that unit. Through the life of Shawna, we will see that this God given Soul Tie extends beyond space and time, and ties every life within the family to one another.

We received a call late one evening telling us that our granddaughter had just died. No explanation, no cause or reason why, just that she had died. As my husband hung up the phone from the conversation, all I felt was pure anger and rage. Not anger or hurt that we weren't given any information on how this happened, just a strange anger that I just didn't understand and it seemed to be almost a "righteous indignation" that came over me. It would be several years before I would gain understanding over these sudden feelings. I prayed, I cried for days, and still I could not get any peace or relief from the rage and anger that I was feeling. It wasn't grief over our granddaughter's death, it wasn't compassion for our child that had this happen to them it was just pure anger raging inside of me. Finally, the anger subsided, I resolved myself to the fact that one day I would see my granddaughter in heaven, and then I would understand. I also made a commitment that I would never forget Shawna while on this earth either, whenever anyone would ask how many grandchildren we had, she was always included in the count.

One day, several years after Shawna's death, I was talking on the phone with a family member, and they began telling me the story about Shawna. They had been there when Shawna was born, and told me that Shawna had been aborted by an abortion pill taken during the pregnancy, that Shawna was actually born alive, and remained alive for two short hours. They also told me that day, Shawna was beautiful, and perfect, however her little eyes were sealed closed. They also told me that they had to make all the funeral arrangements and they paid for the funeral. Now after all these years later, I finally understood why I had felt the anger and rage when we heard of her death. It was because of how Shawna died, by a choice that was made that affected the soul tie within.

12

John Is My Brother

IN LATE WINTER, of 1986, I became pregnant, although I wasn't aware of it yet. I had always wanted more children, and especially I wanted a little boy, to "replace" the little boy that I had been forced to give up for adoption earlier in my life. I already had a name for a little boy that I might have again, and that name was John. Suddenly in early January 1987, I began experiencing extreme pains in the left side of my lower abdomen/pelvic region, and I went to see my doctor. After examining me for quite some time, he determined that I had a tubal pregnancy and he sent me immediately to the hospital without further explanation.

A tubal pregnancy is where the baby is beginning form in the fallopian tube instead of in the uterus of a woman. When this happens, within a few weeks, the woman's tube, which is not designed to gestate a baby, will rupture and will cause not only the baby to die, but the mother as well.

This is why I was experiencing the pain, which was because my fallopian tube was expanding, and almost to the point of rupturing when the doctor had examined me that day. Now with tubal pregnancies that have to be terminated, the doctors make it all seem so doctorfied by calling it an ordinary procedure called a D-N-C. They explain that what they will do is go in and scrape the uterus walls, and remove all the tissue....blah,blah,blah...however, my doctor further explained that he was also going to evacuate my fallopian tubes, and he said, "and I will almost guarantee you that once I clean you out you will be pregnant again within 6 weeks." What he neglected to say was that he was actually doing a medically necessary abortion. Now maybe he was trying not to use the word abortion, or whatever his reasons were I don't know, but I went through the process and was released from the hospital within a day or two.

Now, as far as I was concerned I had just lost a baby, and my emotions were all over the place as you might expect. We went to my in-laws house just to get away for a couple of weeks, and there is where my meltdown happened. I cried, and cried for days, laid on the floor in the fetal position and couldn't believe that I had killed my baby. It really didn't matter at that point that had I not had the abortion, that it would have killed me, I was just horrified that I had allowed my baby to be killed. I had fought so hard to save my first child from being aborted, and now I have allowed John to be aborted. As the days turned into weeks, I finally regained my composure and zeal for life again, probably because I still had a 4 year old who needed me. Eventually, week six since Johns' abortion came, and sure enough, to the day, I was pregnant with my youngest son Marcus.

When Marcus was about two years old, up until he was about 5 he had what parents usually refer to as an imaginary friend. According to Marcus, his friend's name was John, and many times Marcus would tell me that John was his brother not just a friend. Now at the time I never put two and two together, but over the years, and through my biblical studies, comparative religions studies, and my current ministry I have learned that often times our children's so called imaginary friends are actually their siblings Guardian Angels or even their own Guardian Angels. Marcus' little imaginary friend was in fact his older brother John, who had been aborted 6 weeks before Marcus was conceived. Moreover, for those of you that don't believe what I am talking about, Marcus had no way of knowing anything about my abortion, because we have never discussed this topic with any of our children until the writing of this book.

Though my studies, I have learned of other women that have had miscarriages or abortions, would later hear that their young children after their miscarriages or abortions would actually have an imaginary friend show up. This is further documented all over the internet now days, and actually, the Catholic religion has understood the spiritual aspects and the ministry of angels for centuries. The bible actually talks about the ministries of angels however, we as Christians seem to overlook those scripture as somehow being "Spooky Spiritual" and don't want to even think of the possibility that God would have provided spiritual beings, ones often not seen in our lives to assist us. So my advice to parents is don't be alarmed that you child may have an imaginary friend, but do be on the lookout for the possible demonic imaginary friend that might try to enter your child's life, because there are always two sides in the Spiritual realm, Good and Evil.

13

Amy's Fragments

MANY TIMES, PEOPLE who have had traumatic childhood experiences, their brains and I truly believe God Grace and Mercy causes us to repress those memories and experiences until we are able to deal with them and be set free from the vise grip they have held on our lives. Often times what will happen in these cases is that the victim of such horrible abuses will one day have a trigger pulled or some say a light switch is turned on and the rush of memories that were so deeply embedded within one's own mind suddenly snaps into hyper-drive and the wave of memories, and emotions come flooding in much like a tidal wave crashing upon the sandy shores of the beach. You can't stop it you just have to roll with it. In addition, those closest to us must be prepared to allow the emotions to flow, and just be there to help gather the fragments as they come flooding forth. Such is the case in Amy's life.

While interviewing Amy for another chapter for this book, I soon realized that there was much more to Amy's life than just the death of her infant son, which you will read about later in chapter 15. Graciously, Amy has allowed me to share some of her story, so that you might receive hope and healing through whatever difficulties or traumas you might be dealing with. While I am only going to share some of the outskirts of her life that are relevant to the topic of this book, there is much more that Amy will share when she writes the rest of her story in her own books someday.

Amy's story begins as a child from a very broken and dysfunctional home, but she wouldn't come to realize just how dysfunctional for many years. Amy was a straight "A" student, did all the classic "good student" activities, and was extremely popular among her peers. That being said, without warning, one day during her first year of high school her world would come crashing down on top of her and life, as she knew it would never be the same. She was in the school library one day and found a book on adult survivors of sexual abuse, which to this day she doesn't understand why that book was in a school library. As she was looking through the book, and reading some of the stories within that book, her life began to unravel, one thread at a time and all the pieces that held her life together broke into the multitudes of fragments that have now become her life.

As she walked out of the library that day, her world came crashing down, and a dear friend of hers found her on the floor of the hallway, screaming, crying, and lying in the fetal position on the floor. This friend picked Amy's shattered, fragmented body up off the floor, and carries her like a helpless baby to the nurse's office to get her some much-needed help. As Amy and her friend sit in front of the counselor sitting behind the desk, the counselors face is simply white with shock and disbelief as to what is happening with Amy. At the young age of 15 Amy has now had her first emotional breakdown, all the repressed memories of a traumatized life have now come crashing in on her, and all she is left with is fragments.

Over the course of the next several years, Amy's life would spiral downward into failing grades, substance abuse, as well as having to continue to live in a dysfunctional and abusive home environment. Victims in abusive situations, have to be removed from the abuse before any help or healing can occur. If they are not removed from the abusive environment, they will begin to have the pile up syndrome experience as I call it, where shattered fragments upon shattered fragment just pile up upon one another and what you are left with is a pile much like a puzzle that has been dumped out onto the floor and you simply don't know where to begin to start gathering the fragments. As the pile of fragments build up, the victim will simply try to sweep them under the rug of their minds and try to carry on life as if everything is ok, until one day the rug explodes again much like an erupting volcano this time, causing destruction and completely destroying the innocent life that was stolen so early.

Human beings are good at sweeping thing under the rug, however we never realize that the bulging mound underneath will soon erupt and we won't know when or the amount of devastation it will cause. Classic symptoms of coping with the ever-growing bulge are self-destructive behaviors such as; substance abuse, anger issues, depression, disassociation disorders of all kinds, anti-social behavior issues, and the most dangerous of all is the denial that anything is wrong. We will walk around the growing mounds, we might even try to make the pile into a piece of modern art décor in our minds eye for our life somehow thinking that it will just go away one day. Amy put it so appropriately during our interview when she said: "You have to allow the emotions to flow; just like the milk in your breast must be expressed, so do your emotions. If you don't express the emotions they will cause great pain and physical harm."

Amy's drug of choice was prescription drugs, and given Amy's emotional history, many doctors had no problem with prescribing drugs that numb or dull the pain, instead of digging deeper into the real causes for the need to numb or dull the emotional pains. Emotional pain can and will manifest into real physical pain and if it isn't dealt with properly, can be a cause of death. Please don't miss understand me, doctors are many times instruments that God uses to heal us of physical issues, however scientists have also proven that emotional pain will result in physical harm to the body, and many times doctors will try to medicate the problems away, when what is really needed is the freedom from the source of the pain. This is why so many people that have abuse in their backgrounds try to self-medicate to ease the pain. Amy's pain was being medicated by doctors that were unwilling or not aware of the symptoms of abuse, and consequently kept refilling her meds as a way to help her cope, she told me that each time she would take her pills as she was putting them into her mouth, she would continually say to herself, "I don't know why I keep taking these" and down would go one, two or even three more pills, just trying to dull the pain that she was experiencing.

The years would roll forward, and suddenly Amy found a loving caring God, who would begin to help her gather the fragments of her life and place them upon the Cross that Jesus Died upon to set her free. Just recently, the Holy Spirit revealed to Amy that one of the issues that she had been repressing and carrying with her all these years was that she had become pregnant by an abuser connected to her family. She had been taken to have an abortion at an earlier age and the trauma was simply too great for such an innocent mind to comprehend and those memories hadn't surfaced until just recently when she was be able to handle them, and release them to her Heavenly Father. Many times we will be given dreams in our sleep that are directly from God, trying to reveal areas of our life that we need to be healed or set free of, however we often times chalk them up to being "Pizza Dreams" or just really bad nightmares and trash them as not important. Place the fragments of your life, your dreams, your nightmares upon Jesus' cross and Freedom Will Rein!

#4 Points To Ponder

IN THESE DAYS and times, we are constantly bombarded by Pro Life verse Pro Choice demonstrations, outraged individuals and wildly out of control tantrums. What both of these groups fail to notice or realize at times is that there are actual people connected to their hate speeches and taunts. The Christian Pro Life groups of people carrying signs with hate messages inscribed on them, which further traumatizes any person that has had an abortion without a safe place to begin to heal from their traumas. The Pro Choice groups, demanding their rights to make choices about their own bodies, only further traumatize individuals by telling them that it's a choice and not a baby, are totally missing the point that abortion is murder since we have learned that life begins at conception and these people are actually calling something evil a good thing.

Please don't miss understand me, I am Pro Life however I don't believe that we need to beat people over the head about the choices that they make that are against our beliefs and understanding. We need to learn that Love is always going to take the higher road in this issue realizing that there are people that need our love, not our condemnation. I was once one of these people that were very vocal about my condemnation of anyone who would will have an abortion simply because it was inconvenient to have a baby, or they had a one–night stand and forgot to use protection. I have since taken on the side of love, which wants to lovingly care about the people that have become victims of the choices that they have made. The reason that I call them victims is because that is exactly what they are. The survivors of abortions are the women and men that made that choice to abort a child and now even years later are still struggling to find peace over the choices that they had made. These choices are actually tormenting thousands of individuals, who are hurting in silence because to come out or confess what they have done sets them up for condemnation from the very people that they are often looking for comfort from.

I have counseled many women who seemed to be stuck in their life, and keep making the same bad decisions repeatedly throughout their life without ever knowing why. The problem is that our lives are much like a CD that has a scratch in on it, when it reaches the same point on the disk, it skips and begins playing the same verse or chorus again, never able to get past the scratch. What we need is someone willing to step into our life, wipe the CD clean, and restore the disk to its original unscratched condition. That person is Jesus, who is the only true life CD cleaner and restorer, and Christians are to be Jesus with skin on, assisting those people with the restoration process.

The other point that I need to make is that in order to be set free from the abuses of the past as the bible puts it, Confess your sins (issues) one to another so that you may be healed. The enemy of your soul wants you to remain locked within your abusive past, much like keeping you locked behind prison doors without a key. Or another way to think about it is that often times we have skeletons in the closet of our perfect little lives that we so try hard to cover up, actually the skeletons that we are wanting to keep hidden in the closet, are keeping you in bondage and fear of somehow they will come tumbling out and your shame, and ugly past that you have been trying to keep neatly tucked away, are soon discovered by others.

The reality is that free people can see when we have skeletons, and truly free people want to help you clear out the clutter and bondage in your life. Jesus has the keys to your freedom and has handed those keys to you so that freedom will be allowed to step in when you begin to open up and to share your experiences with someone whom you can trust and that you know loves and cares for you. At first, that person may only be Jesus through prayer behind a closed door, but later, you will find that God will bring others across your path with which you can share your situation and story with, and the more that you begin to bring your story into the light of God's love, the freer you will be. Freedom is a progressive thing, the longer you allow God to work in your life, the freer you will become. Just as there are lessons to be learned through our life experiences, so to there are life lessons that we will only learn through the death of a child in our lives, regardless of whether that death was from an abortion that we had in our past or a child that has died at the onset of their life, they all have lessons and golden God nuggets hidden deep within, if we are willing to open our hearts and let the love of God shine upon them and unearth the nuggets of these lives.

Section V

Miscarriage Of Expectation

John 10:7–10

Then Jesus said to them again, "Most assuredly, I say to you, I am the door of the sheep. All who ever came before Me are thieves and robbers, but the sheep did not hear them. I am the door. If anyone enters by Me, he will be save, and will go in and out and find pasture. The thief does not come except to steal, and to kill, and to destroy. I have come that they may have life, and that they may have it more abundantly."

14

Tobi's Birth Meant Death

JOANN JUST NEWLY pregnant with their 10th child, set out to find a new home that her and Ferris could call the homestead. This new home had to accommodate not only their current 8 surviving children, but all of the others that Joann and Ferris were sure to come. They always knew that they wanted lots of children, and now the time came that they needed a home that was large enough for their growing family. They were living in the Waxahachie/Midlothian area of Texas at the time and really liked the rural setting in which to raise their children and wanted to remain in this community. As with anyone looking for a new home the first place you start is to find a local realtor, and begin the search. As Joann and the realtor began touring the available homes in the area, and as small talk about their family came about, the realtor realizes that Joann and Ferris have 8 children, and she is now pregnant with another. Without warning, the realtor asks Joann, "And none of your children have any birth defects?" Joann thinking "what a weird question" responded Of course I don't have children with any birth defects, and in her mind she was thinking, "I don't smoke, I don't do drugs, I eat super healthy, why would I have a baby with a birth defect?"

Joann's pregnancy with Tobi was flawless as far as pregnancies go, and she dismissed the day's conversation with the realtor and her weird question, and carried on looking for their new home. Everything seemed right with Joann's pregnancy, and even the visits to the Mid-wife went flawlessly. One day while just doing a routine self-examine, which is common with women who use a Mid-wife to deliver their children, Joann noticed that for some reason she was unable to palpitate the baby's head, but that really didn't seem that strange to her because it could be the baby is just turned in such a way that she was unable to locate the head. On the next visit to the Mid-wife, Joann and Julia joked and laughed about the fact that this baby moves around so much that Joann told Julia that she was having a hard time palpitating the baby's head. They each laughed and made some comments about the acrobatics of the baby and the visit ended without any complications.

Little did Joann know that her Mid-wife, Julia was concerned about the fact that she too was having difficulty in palpitating the baby's head during the pre-natal visits, but was not showing that concern to her, to keep from needless alarming Joann at this point. Another thing that Joann was unaware of about Julia was that just a year earlier, Julia had another patient that had delivered an anencephalic baby, and Julia knew that the odds of seeing another anencephalic baby was so great that there was no way this could be another one. In the meantime, Joann was having some very disturbing thoughts that something just seemed not quite right about this pregnancy, but she kept pushing those thoughts aside, never discussed her troubling thoughts to anyone, and never discussed them with Julia. Either did Joann remember the conversation several months prior with the realtor, or maybe this was just the seeds of that conversation set to assail her mind during this pregnancy.

One day during Joann's normal final month of pre-natal visits with Julia, Julia suggested to her that they should have a sonogram done, Julia didn't say why, and Joann didn't ask. Joann, simply agreed immediately, and so Julia scheduled the appointment for the next weeks' visit. The morning of the sonogram finally had arrived, and Joann really felt that Ferris should come to the appointment with her. This was unusual for Joann, since Ferris had never been to any of her previous doctor or Mid-Wife appointments, because, in Joann's words; "He is a working guy, we needed the money, and I took care of all this stuff." However, this time, Joann really believed that Ferris needed to come with her, and she was shocked that Ferris immediately agreed. Joann thought that she might have to talk him into going, but much to her surprise, Ferris was already to go with her that day.

As the results of the sonogram were given to them, they have now become the parents of an anencephalic baby, whose only outcome was certain death upon birth. The sonogram revealed that Tobi's skull was not developed past the hairline, and all that was there was brain tissue on the top of her head. Joann said; "We were totally devastated by this news, and I was so angry that I had to practice saying the word Anencephalic in order to tell the rest of the family what was happening. I mean I was really, angry, and that country song on the radio Stop the World and let me off was exactly what I felt like. I knew from already having lost one baby what we were in for, and how incredible emotionally draining this was going to be, and I was just dreading it, complete and utter dread just engulfed me." Now Joann and her family were going to have to work through this. This was going to be different from their other child that they lost, because now they know that Tobi's birth means death. This wasn't going to be a sudden happening like with Misty, but it was going to be a month long journey of knowing that as soon as labor begins with Tobi, her end would be drawing near.

Julia, Joann's Mid-wife told her, "If you want me to deliver this baby, I am available." However, Joann being the kind and gentle hearted soul that she is knew that this was going to be a traumatic experience for everyone involved, and knowing that Julia had just been through this experience with another friend of hers Joann didn't want to put Julia through this trauma again. Therefore, Joann with her planning nature in full force set out to find a doctor that would deliver Tobi when the time came. She soon found out that doctors don't want to deliver a "bad baby", and no one was interested in seeing her in her condition, and Joann said "nor do they want to touch you with a ten foot pole" and the same response kept coming, 'just go to the ER when the time comes'. Finally, Joann, against her better judgment contacted the doctor that had delivered 3 of the other children, and was the doctor that had delivered Misty, since he did understand that Joann wanted to have all her children naturally, without any medications or sedatives to see what he said. He agreed he would deliver Tobi when the time come, and began telling Ferris and Joann

"You know, these babies are usually stillborn, they are born dead, and that's the way that we like it".

Now Joann and Ferris have finally found a doctor that would deliver Tobi when the time comes, and as they walked to the car to go home, Joann told Ferris, "I'm having this baby at home, and Ferris quickly agreed, yes, we are having her at home." Now Joann understood what the doctor was saying, but she said, "It just went all wrong on me, and especially since he was the one that had delivered Misty, and I was kind of putting that little statement in with Misty's situation, and decided, Oh, no, no we aren't going through that again". As they got into the car, Joann said that a sudden wave of Peace had come over her as she decided that they were going to have this baby at home. After arriving home, they called Julia, the mid-wife, and told her that if she would still consider delivering this baby when the time comes that they had decided that Tobi needed to be born around people who would be sad at her passing, and show compassion when she was gone, not relief. Julia agreed without hesitation, and scheduled Joann for her next pre-natal checkup.

One of the common problems that women with Anencephalic babies in the womb experience is tremendous water weight gain. The reason for this is that Anencephalic babies tend not to swallow the amniotic flu that surrounds them and thus causes the fluid to build up and not be expelled as with normal babies. This results in a build up the fluid that causes extreme discomfort for the mother, and the surrounding organs of her body. Joann, said, "I was only able to eat about a tablespoon of food at any one time, and at times was having a hard time breathing because I was retaining all this water weight. We had to do something, because I felt like I was starving Tobi, by not being able to eat, or breathe well." So when Joann went in for her checkup about a week before her due date, Julia and she discussed what options they had to try to alleviate some of the amniotic fluid. Julia agreed that something had to be done and suggested that they go in and try to break her water just a little bit, to try to give her some relief.

Joann and Ferris return home to prepare everything for the impending breaking of the waters, and Tobi's arrival. "We knew that there would be a lot of water, but we were not prepared for what happened." When Julia arrived and broke Joann's water, water gushed forth, so much water in fact that Joann immediately lost 21 pounds, which equates to almost 3 gallons of water. Immediately Joann had relief, and contractions soon followed. Now the time had come that Joann had dreaded for the last month or so....Tobi's birth which meant Tobi's death.

Now that the waters have been broken, and the fact that Tobi is an anencephalic baby, normal delivery in now more complicated. The reason for the complicated delivery is that in Anencephalic babies, since the head or skull is not formed, it doesn't have the hard surface in which to cause the cervix to dilate as in a normal birth. In hospital deliveries, a doctor will a lot of times deliver these children by C-section simply because either the waters broke too soon, or the mother's cervix are not dilating as they should, or the being of labor is taking too long. Joann having a home birth has to force the birth of Tobi, without many of the same sensations that a normal birth would have. Joann said; "I had to decide in my head that I'm going to birth this baby, I'm going to push this baby out. The biggest problem that I had was mentally I knew that birth meant death, and that just kept ringing in my head over and over as I am trying to birth this baby." Joann was hopeful that Tobi would be born alive, just to see life in her eye if only for a second, Joann believed that would somehow help her through the traumatic days ahead.

About Midnight the night of that labor had begun for Joann, an unknown visitor came to the door of the house and left a small little bag for caring for the baby when she arrived. This person did not identify herself, however they did know that she was a neo-natal nurse of one of the very large hospitals around town because of the badges that hung around her neck. However, to this day, no one knows whom that woman was or how she came to know where or when Tobi was being born, but she had a gift of love to give to this precious little one upon arrival. Joann, learning that someone from the outside had come by at midnight just to give them a gift to help care for her baby touches her heart in an unbelievable way, and somehow gives her renewed strength to birth Tobi.

In the early morning hours Tobi is finally born, however she is stillborn, so Joann hoping to see a little life in her eyes was not to be. The mid-wife determined by the discoloration of Tobi's face that she had died sometime within a couple of hours of her birth. Joann wrapped the baby up, and allowed the other children to come in and say their goodbyes. Each child in their turn touched little Tobi's hand, and sent her off to heaven with their love and admiration for their little sister. Now, the rest of the family leaves Joann alone with Tobi so that she can say her goodbyes, and Joann said, "She rocked Tobi and held her close for about an hour, until she was ready to let her go." She had made a little basket for Tobi while she was pregnant with her, and placed Tobi in the basket and placed perfume all over the basket just to show Tobi how much she was loved and cared for. Now for the next process of having Tobi declared dead.

With home births, the mid-wife cannot declare a child dead that can only be done by either a Judge, or a medical doctor. Joann's family first called a lady Judge in town to see if she would make the declaration of death, and she immediately tells them "No, we will have to preform and autopsy to determine how the child died, and the exact cause of death, and take that baby to the hospital or county morgue, and they will perform the procedure." Well, neither Joann, Ferris or the mid-wife see the need for an autopsy on an Anencephalic baby, and in Joann's words, "It's kind of obvious on why and how the baby died, and NO ONE IS CUTTING ON MY BABY." So finally, they contacted a doctor that they knew pretty well, and asked him if he would complete the declaration of death, and he said, "Yes, just bring her around the back way, and I will make the declaration needed and handle all the legal stuff for you."

As the days pasted after Tobi's birth that meant death, Joann did go through the grief process. She didn't know it at the time, but everyone in the family was grieving and one day Ferris looks at her as and says, "We have all these other kids right now, I think that it is time that this is the last one." Joann instantly says, "Oh, NO, I'm going out on a bad note like this, there is NO WAY, this is going to be the last one." She said that if she had stopped having children at this point that would have been the death of her as well, she doesn't like going out on a bad note, and she wasn't going to start now! Within the next couple of days, she contacted her Mid-wife and asked her advice on how long she should wait before having another baby. Julia said, "Joann, you are healthy, and you can have another baby anytime you want to have another baby", and this was just what Joann wanted to hear, so within the next few months she would be pregnant with child number 11, about 6 months after Tobi.

As Joann reflects back on Tobi's birth, she recalls the lessons that she learned through her pregnancy with Tobi, Tobi's birth that meant certain death, and how Yahweh's hand was there through every step of the process. Joann said that as she looks back, "Yahweh had been preparing me for this so I could handle it. He didn't let me find out that Tobi was Anencephalic when I was only three months pregnant he waited until just before she was born to let me find out. If I had known throughout the entire pregnancy that would have been a burden, I don't know if I could have been able to bear had I known. Yahweh, gave me just enough time to deal with the anger, the pain, and allowed time for Peace to be ushered in to get me through the processes to come." "Yahweh was so faithful to send and keep angels around me throughout this entire process, from my angel of a Mid-wife, to the angel who at midnight brought such a loving gift of compassion and care when Tobi was born. I can see that His Hand was guiding all along the way, to see that Tobi was born into a room for loving, caring, compassionate people that created such the right atmosphere for Tobi to be born into." Also, Joann remembers after Tobi was born, the realtor's weird question of "And none of them have birth defects", and believes that Yahweh was first teaching her just how arrogant she really was about thinking that she was in control, when it was Him that is in control, and that she needed not to think that if she did everything right, that was the reason that none of her children had any birth defects of any kind. The second thing that she believes that she learned through this process was that you are not to judge whether someone has done something wrong just because something bad has happened to them, YOU are NOT in control and are not allowed to be judgmental on any situations around you! The final lesson that Joann would like to share with others is that Medical books will put fear into your hearts about your situation that you are going through, yes learn about the situation but allow Yahweh to give you Peace through the situation.

15

The Resurrection Life Of Ike

THE INTERNET AGE has many attributes good and bad, but the best attribute is that the Internet age can help authors find ordinary people who have a story that can be helpful to others. Such a story is the following story of the resurrection life of Ike. Thanks in part to "Facebook", and friends of friends of whom we both have attended church with, I met Amy, and learned that she had a story that would fit beautifully in this book. As an author and a pastor, I am continually looking for stories of ordinary people that have overcome extraordinary situations, and have lessons to share with others that may be going through similar situations in their lives. I believe that the testimonies of others on how God has brought them through some the most difficult situations in their lives need to be written and shared with as many people as it possibly can so that we don't feel quite as alone in this cold cruel world. I also want to show others just how God turns every evil thing that the devil tries to do in a person life, and He works it for their good and brings hope to others.

As we all know who are on any social networks, we are connected often times with friends of friends, and we accept friendships with others just because they happen to be mutual friends with someone that we know. I believe that this is often referred to as six degrees of separation and you can find anyone and be connected with anyone in the world through others that you know. Such is how this story began for me. Several of my church friends were very upset on June 7, 2010, and I began to inquire what had happened. A dear friend of mine told me that a family in the Church had just lost their infant son, but the associate pastor told everyone not to contact the family. Then I turned to another close friend and previous co-worker at the church to inquire further on the situation and find out some more details since this person was a friend of mine on "Facebook", and I wanted to find out what if anything I could possibly do. She said that she thought that this family had come to the church after I had left to start my ministry, and wasn't sure if I knew them or not. I told her yes but I only knew them through being friends on "Facebook". Therefore, the only thing I could do for this family was to pray, and pray I did. As a pastor, I know that one of the worst things that a family can go through is the death of a child, and I know the stats on families surviving the death of a child are very small due to the high stress factors involved. Therefore, I began saying a daily prayer over this family every morning for about a week, "Lord, bring healing and restore hope, supply them with Resurrection Life, and fill their hearts with your peace, your peace that passes all understanding, and show yourself mighty in this family, in Jesus name Amen". After a week, the need for daily prayer over this family left me, and my spiritual attachment seemed to wane as well.

The morning of July 4, 2010, the Lord woke me up telling me that it was time for me to start writing my first book that He had been talking to me for years to write. I asked Him, what is the title of the book, and He said "A Life of Significance". My immediate response was; "and what is it supposed to be about since I know that all our lives are significant to you". His response was "I want you to write a book that details the lives of ordinary people that have had planned or unplanned pregnancies, people who have adopted children into their families or given up child for adoption, people who have had an abortion by choice or by medical necessity, and I also want you to include families that have had children stolen by death, and through all these people lives you will show just how significant their lives are to me and to others around them." Moreover, immediately I felt like Moses, and began to say, I can't write about those subjects, I don't have any experience in every area that you are talking about.

I did not hear another word from the Lord on the subject of the book that I was to write until, July 29, 2010 when he directed me to make a post on my "Facebook" page to find people that would be willing to share their personal stories for a book. The people willing to share their stories and testimonies were incredible and one response I received I would not realize the significance of for another year when I would begin to write this story. Amy was one of the responses to my search on July 30, 2010, only a little more than a month since her infant son died in his sleep, and I would not connect the two until I began to write this chapter of the book of which you are about to read.

The book seemed to lag at this point and I was beginning to wonder if I had heard the Lord correctly that I would complete this book, however, I do know that sometimes the Lord will tell us the things that we are to do, and it is as if He has to allow us time to get use to the idea of what he has called us to do, and also, time for the other parties involved to come to terms with assisting us in our projects. You see God never only works with one end of a miracle at a time He is always working on all ends of the miracle at the same time so that we can complete the tasks in His time and with His intended purposes.

At the onset of the interview with Amy waiting to hear how significant Ike's life was in only two short months, one of the first comments that she made was; "I know that this is going to sound strange, but I believe that Ike's death actually saved my marriage and family", now I am totally taken back by her comment, and completely undone with what I know as a pastor that most marriages that experience the death of a child usually end in divorce from the stresses involved by losing a child, and here I have a woman that is telling me that her son's death actually saved her marriage and their family. I was so completely taken back by her first comment, that all my questions flew out the window, and I had to just allow her to begin to talk about anything and everything that she wanted to share with me regarding Ike, her family, her pregnancy with Ike, etc.... then I would find the ray of light, and hope that myself and you the reader need to see in learning just how significant Ike's life was wrapped up in only two short months.

As our interview continued, after regaining my composure somewhat, I began to learn that on June 7, 2010, not only did Ike die that day, but so did their entire family. The world ended that day for this family, and everything was about to change, in ways they could not have possibly known. Amy began sharing with me that because of Ike's death, hidden things within their marriage began to come to light. This reminded me of the scripture in the Bible that everything hidden will be brought into the light. I didn't inquire any deeper into the hidden things since I know that some things don't need to be shared in a public forum, and wasn't relevant to the Resurrection Life of Ike, other than to know that EVERYTHING was brought out into the light, through the death of Ike. I learned that even their friendships have changed over the course of the last year since Ike's death. Amy said that she had only one friend that she had had since childhood and that was the only friend that lasted through the process. Everyone else either didn't know what to say or would make ignorant statements on how or why Ike died. The one thing that she wanted me to share with those of you that might be going through a similar situation is "Don't get lost in the stupid things that people might say to you, simply because they don't know what to say at a time like this, people mean well, but can really say some of the dumbest things."

Ike was born premature, because of a medical condition that Amy had, and was born at 33 weeks. One of the warnings that the doctors gave them was that Sudden Infant Death Syndrome, SIDS, is a common concern with premature births, and one that needed a close eye kept out for. Ike was exceeding expectations at every turn, and by the time he was 6 weeks old he had not only regained his birth weight but had actually doubled it, and was doing exceptionally well for being born prematurely. On the morning of June 7, 2010, Amy woke up at 5 a.m., and walked into the kitchen to get Ike's bottle ready since it had appeared that he had slept through the night for the first time. After getting his bottle prepared, she walked into Ike's room to check on him, and found that he was not breathing. She called 911, and began CPR until the paramedics arrived. Her husband was out of town on a job assignment, so she had to call him and tell him what had happened and that he needed to come home. She was also the one that had to tell the other children what had happened to their baby brother. Through the entire process of having to explain to her husband and other children in the home what had happened to Ike, she was also enduring a police investigation regarding the circumstance surrounding Ike's sudden and unexpected death. Truly, an all-consuming fire was running through their family and household burning up everything they had ever known to be their so-called life and marriage.

I have never been so awe struck at the hand of God over a situation before this story of Ike crossed my path. Ike's life truly has brought resurrection life to not only this family and their marriage but has brought resurrection life to me personally having been allowed the awesome privilege of having a small part in this story. I know that through my small daily prayers of resurrection life over this family has influenced not only their life but yours too since reading this story. I didn't go into all the details surrounding this story, because it would require many, many books to write all the lessons learned by this family, and is their story to share later. The point of including it in this book is to show God's marvelous handy work in bringing many people together to create the miracles that he wants perform in each one of our lives. Also, to show us that truly what the devil means for our harm, God can and will turn it for our good, no matter how it may look to you or those around you. I believe also, this book could not have been written without this story, and had to be a work in progress for over the last year, so that I personally could learn a much-needed lesson on waiting on God to finish the task that he had given to me over a year ago. Ike's life definitely qualifies as "A Life of Significance" in many ways, and I believe that the Lord is looking down upon each of us and smiling as we learn that no matter the length of a life all lives are significance, and sometime we need to learn to look beyond the surface of a situation to find His hidden nuggets of gold in the mist of chaos!

#5 Points To Ponder

Events such as stillbirths, early or late miscarriages, and even the deaths of our children are a miscarriage of our expectations. With every pregnancy, we carry a certain amount of expectations about the birth and development of our children. We expect them to be born, perfect little human beings, to grow up strong, go to college, get married, and have their own children for us to spoil rotten in our golden years. However, sometimes, our expectations are thwarted, and we don't understand why, and actually only God knows why, and hasn't provided us a clear understanding and won't until we get to Heaven. We can however learn lessons from the Golden God nuggets that each life contains, whether it was shortened by miscarriage or death, and many times we can learn life lessons through the death process that we would not have learned any other way unfortunately. Life and Death are all part of the circle of life, and provide us with their own lessons to be learned, and nuggets to be gathered.

Such was the case in the previous two chapters on Tobi and Ike. These lives were cut short tragically; however, they were lives that contain valuable golden nuggets for the parents, and others to glean. The parents of Tobi learned that they were far too arrogant to expect that since they lived a "perfect life" and did all the right things in their life how could they ever have a child born with any birth defects. Tobi's life also gave Joann compassion for other parents of children with birth defect that she hadn't had until Tobi was stillborn. Tobi also gave Joann a resolve that she wouldn't give up on having any more children just because of this one bad experience either, which I believe was a strength that came only through Tobi's short life in the womb that was transfer to Joann through the umbilical cord that attached them to each other. Through that umbilical cord flowed nutrients for life to Tobi from Joann, and strength and resolve for life was flowing to Joann from Tobi. Ike on the other hand, through his death brought resurrection life to the entire family. Amy shared that there were many hidden sins that were unearthed and discovered within their marriage that had Ike not died actually would have allowed those sins and hidden things to remain hidden.

Whenever parents unexpectedly lose a child, often times the first attack is on the trust of each of the partners within the marriage, and the "what ifs" and accusations begin to fly. This is the biggest reason why marriages of parents that suddenly lose a child often end in divorce, because actually the death has unearthed some unresolved feelings of insecurity between the husband and wife. If we would learn that actually, the hidden things that surface through this process are a cleansing process, actually meant to help us survive through it. However, as is so often the case with human nature, we want someone to blame for this event, and it can never be ourselves and we are never happy with "it just happens sometimes", it always has to be someone else's fault. Many times the next person that we begin to blame is God. Let me let you in on a secret, God didn't do this to punish you for something, and God is not in the killing business. It is actually the enemy of your soul who seeks only to kill, steal and destroy, not God, and so really if you want to get right down to it, the person that you should be blaming is the devil for bringing death into the Garden of Eden all those thousands of years ago.

Life is a spiritual fight, and not a fight against flesh and blood. We can though, through the death of a loved one can find the Golden God Nuggets that God has deposited for us through that life, if we are willing mine them out instead of allowing the enemy to destroy everyone surrounded to that life. The most important thing to remember as you continue reading through the next section is that Jesus gave us these words; John 10:10 – "the thief does not come except to steal, and to kill, and to destroy. I have come that they may have life, and that they may have it more abundantly", and Paul tells us in Romans 8:28 – "And we know that all things work together for good to those who love God, to those who are the called according to His purpose." The death of your child was not done by God, but God will use the life and death of your loved one, to work for your good by providing you His Golden nuggets not hidden from you, but hidden FOR YOU TO FIND!

Section VI

Stolen Lives And The Blessings That They Leave Behind

Romans 8:28–30

In addition, we know that all things work together for good to those who love God, to those who are the called according to His purpose. For whom He foreknew, He also predestined to be conformed to the image of His Son, that He might be the firstborn among many brethren. Moreover, whom He predestined, these He also called; whom He called, these He also justified; and whom He justified, and these He also glorified.

16

Misty Lynn's Legacy

FERRIS AND JOANN were married very young in life, Joann was 15 almost 16 years old, and this couple was truly in love. They weren't getting married because they "had to", they got married because, they had found their life's love, and wanted to begin their life as a couple. Joann wouldn't get pregnant for almost three years after their marriage. Joann always knew that she wanted children, and lots of them, and this is probably why this couple wanted to begin their adult life as soon as they did, because they were following Yahweh's plans for their life, and not their own.

Having been married for some time, Ferris and Joann became increasingly concerned that they would not be able to have the children that they so desperately desired, and knew that they wanted to bring into this life and love of theirs. In Joann's words, "I always knew I wanted children, that was just who I was". However, time went on, they learned that Joann had a cousin that was born without a uterus, and her older sister had been married for years, and had never been able to conceive, so naturally, since Ferris and Joann hadn't conceived yet, they began to wonder, and be a little concerned. So at the young age of 16 or 17 years old, Joann sets out to learn everything she could about infertility, and she was soon on her way to figuring it all out. Obviously, they didn't need to worry, and Yahweh had it under complete control. Misty is Ferris and Joann's second bundle of joy to arrive into their life, only 1 year and 8 days after their first child had arrived. The following story is Misty's legacy to this very large and most humble family that you would ever want to meet. In talking to others that know this family, they all said that all of the children in this family are the best kids that you would ever want to meet, and the parents are the most humble and REAL people you would ever be privileged to know.

Joann recalls that her pregnancy with Misty had been a good and easy pregnancy to this point, and there was no reason for any concern. Joann does remember that for some reason she was having "panic attacks" and back then we didn't even have a word for "panic attacks" nor did we know what a panic attack was. All she knew is that she would have trouble sleeping and all she felt was sheer panic and aggravation over something she didn't know or understand. Ferris and Joann decided to go on a family vacation with Ferris' mom, dad and one of his sisters to Canada in the summer of 1975. While on vacation, Joann got very ill, with something like the flu. She had a very high fever, chills, and was just generally very sick and very pregnant. While still on vacation in Bath, Canada, Joann's water breaks. Joann says; "We were not wealthy people by any stretch and I did not see how we could afford to have a baby in Canada. So we loaded up the car, and we headed home". Ferris drove the family straight through from Bath, Canada to Cisco Texas, non-stop, and all the way Joann could feel that the baby was right there ready to be born. Joann tells Ferris, "Let just drive as far as we can and if we have to pull off and stop at a hospital somewhere we will, but let's try to make it home". They arrived home late at night, and went to bed for a few hours sleep. The next morning they went to see Joann's doctor, and after examining her, said; "Oh my, this baby is right here, I feel a foot, get to the hospital now!" They arrived at the hospital and it was still several more hours before the baby would be born.

Misty was finally born, almost 3 months early, at 2 pounds 9 ounces, but didn't have any of the ordinary problems that premature babies usually have. Her lungs were fully developed and functioning well, and her heart was functioning, as it should without any issue typical of a premature baby. Joann said, "What I have learned since Misty's birth is that often times, when the mother becomes very ill during her pregnancy, the development of the baby is sped up, due to the fact that the baby may have to be born prematurely." Yahweh's little safety procedure goes into action, to protect the life and health of the unborn child.

Ferris and Joann problems weren't that they had a premature baby; their problem was that they had delivered their premature baby at a very small country hospital, with a staff that was ill equipped to handle such a delicate and fragile life such as Misty. The only issues that Misty really had from being born so prematurely was that she weighed only 2 pounds 9 ounces, and did not have the sucking reflex needed to receive the nourishment that she needed to thrive.

The staff placed Misty into an incubator, and the feeding schedule was every other hour. Initially after Misty's birth, Joann was up and down the hospital hallways, checking in on her newborn through the nursery window. She said that she was in great shape after her birth, and only had concerns for how Misty was doing. During one of her visits to the nursery to stand outside the nursery window, there was a nurse's aide mopping the floor behind Joann as she stood staring in at Misty. The nurse walks up behind Joann, and tells her, "You know what that baby needs?" Joann replies, "No, what does she need?" the nurse's aide, replies, "She needs you to be in there holding her!" "You tell them that you want to go in there and that you want to take care of your baby." Joann, now in complete shock that she could actually demand to care for her baby, and grateful that this person to whom she now refers to as an angel, had given her permission to be Misty's mother, and to begin to help her daughter survive and thrive.

The staff agreed to allow Joann in to hold and begin feeding her new little one on the every other hour schedule. Joann said; "It was such a blessing that my mom lived right across the street from the hospital and made so much easier to go to the hospital feed Misty for an hour and come back home to my 1 year old for an hour, and I continued that routine for three weeks. I would continue that routine every day from 7 a.m. until 11 p.m., and figured that the hospital staff was taking the night shift duties." It literally took an hour for each feeding, since Misty didn't have the sucking reflex, Joann had to only allow a single drop at a time to run down Misty's throat, any more than a single drop and Misty would choke because of her lack of ability to suck and swallow like a fully developed infant.

As Joann would soon learn from being on the inside of the nursery with the staff, not only was Misty receiving the loving touch and care that she could give her, but in fact it was the only touch or care that Misty was receiving. One day Joann not understanding why Misty wasn't gaining and thriving as she thought that she should, decided to read the hospital chart that hung on Misty's incubator. Much to Joann's shock and horror, she found out that, the hospital staff was not feeding Misty AT ALL during the nighttime hours, and that in fact the only person caring for Misty was Joann. Joann soon realized that, everything that she was doing during the day was being destroyed by the hospital staff not feeding and caring for Misty in the middle of the night and learns that this is the reason why she is not gaining the weight that she needs to come home.

Since all this and a lot of other crazy stuff surrounding Misty's care, Ferris and Joann actually considered stealing Misty out of the hospital one day, knowing that Misty had a better chance with them at home. Only one thing stop Ferris and Joann from doing this was the one time that Misty was choked during one of her feeding times. That is all that kept Joann from stealing her daughter away from the incompetent doctors and nursing staff of this little country hospital. Finally, some relief came when their primary doctor had to go away for a few days. The relieving doctor immediately saw that Misty needed to be intubated with a feeding tubing and ordered that be done as soon as possible. Now Joann knew that Misty was being cared for properly, and began to rest a little easier. Now came the tape that would hold the tube in place, massive amounts of tape all over Misty's transparent little face. As Joann stood looking in at her little daughter with all this tape covering this fragile little one's transparent skinned little face, a nurse walks up behind Joann and says, "I don't want to be here the day that all that tape is removed, as a matter of fact none of us want to be here for that task." As soon as their regular doctor arrived back from his few days away, out came Misty's feeding tube, and back Joann and Ferris went in to worry and concern for their daughter.

One day Joann arrives at the hospital for Misty's 7 a.m. feeding and finds that the incubator is now off. After that feeding Joann immediately goes home, tells everyone in the family and all her friends that Misty is doing better, the hospital had turned off the incubator, and that means that Misty will soon be able to come home. Joann continues that days feeding schedule, with a renewed hope that soon she would be able to take her new little daughter home, to meet the rest of the family and her older sibling. The next morning upon arriving for that day's 7 a.m. feeding, and now it's been at least 24 hours that Misty's incubator was not on, Joann picking Misty up out of the incubator realizes that Misty seems to be a little cold, or chilled. So being the good mother that Joann is, she wraps little Misty up really well in a receiving blanket and begins feeding her. Just then a nurse walks in and Joann says; "I don't understand it, Misty seem to be a little chilled to be today", the nurse say, well let's see, and suddenly hears the nurse exclaim the worst possible response, "Who turned off this incubator, no wonder this baby seems cold, someone has unplugged the incubator". Joann's heart sinks, now she knows that the incubator hadn't been turned off the day before, because Misty was doing better, in fact, someone had accidentally unplugged Misty's incubator and none of the hospital staff had realized it until now. Indeed, Misty was chilled and cold, which is not a good situation for a premature baby.

About three days later, after one of the afternoon feedings Joann receives the call that she so desperately didn't want to receive. The person from the hospital on the other end of the phone tells her, "The baby is in trouble". Joann, and the family all race up to the hospital and she had called her husband to get home right away Misty was having trouble. Just after Ferris had arrived, the doctor comes out, tells them that Misty hasn't made it, and is now dead. Their worst fears had come true, and all the family around them, not having ever experienced the loss of a child, didn't know what to say. The family all head home, exhausted from the experience, and Ferris and Joann, go for a drive to try to gather their composure for what lies ahead. During this drive, Joann's concern isn't for herself, having lost a baby, her concern is that she didn't want her younger siblings that were still young and at home to see her pain. She said that she didn't want to inflict any more pain on to them, than what they had already experience. An hour goes by, and while Joann and Ferris are back at home with the family, the phone rings and it's the hospital again, "Joann, the baby just took a big breath and she is alive!" Joann and Ferris run back to the hospital as fast as they could to see their child. All the while, Joann is trying to wrap her head around what is happening to them. "She dead, and now she is alive, what does this mean? Does this mean that Yahweh has given me my child back, and I will never lose her again? Finally, Joann determines, Ok, everything is going to be OK now". After being at the hospital for a while, waiting to hear the doctors report, the hospital staff come out and tells them, that they need to go home, and get some rest, because they need to keep Misty under close observation and to come back in the morning. A few hours later, after everyone had gone to bed for the evening, around 1 a.m. Joann's mother comes into Joann and Ferris' bedroom and tells them, that the hospital just called, and Misty is now dead again.

After all that was done, and left undone, Joann and Ferris never considered filing a lawsuit against the hospital or any of the staff members. Joann said; "Ferris and I were encouraged by several people to sue the hospital and the doctor, and I guarantee you that I was plenty angry enough to have filed, but I was utterly exhausted from the whole ordeal, but suing the hospital would not have brought Misty back. I knew that a lawsuit wouldn't help me heal from this experience, nor would it have made me feel any better about what happened. What this experience did give me was new knowledge, like being set free, knowing when you know something isn't right, it's OK, you don't have to have a name tag or a college education to give you permission to do what is right. That goes for your children or whatever situation that you may find yourself in.

I also learned that I had always been a sympathetic person, feeling sorry for others whenever I heard that they had had some tragedy happen, but from Misty's experience, it was no longer a head empathy that I had for people, it was a heart empathy. Because now I knew more deeply, some of the thoughts and feelings that they were having. This experience also prepared me to look into Home births when I became pregnant with my third child, Josh who was born a year and 2 month after Misty. Now don't get me wrong, if I ever get into trouble or need something that a doctor can help me with I will go ask a doctor, but I don't rely on their name tag and 8 years of college to trust that they know what they are talking about."

Joann had some final thoughts to pass along to others who have or may be experiencing a similar situation:

"Anytime you lose a baby, your next pregnancy is going to be a little traumatic, just because of the situations of the past. One day, you will be healed from this experience one day you will smile again one day will not have those crushing thoughts in your mind. There is going to come one day, when you didn't think about it. You will able to smile, and be normal again. Healing does come, it just takes time." Joann also said, "I believe so strongly that there will be a resurrection that what I determined after I lost Misty, was that I was going to raise all of my children so well, I would instill the highest moral character and values in them, that somehow that will give Misty the greatest chance to prove herself in the resurrection. Just the fact of knowing and believing in the resurrections and the Justice and Fairness of Yahweh, I will see my baby again."

When asked if their other children were raised to know about Misty, Joann said, "YES, children need to learn about life and death. Recently we started a Foundation, and some of the kids suggested that we name it after Tobi and Misty, however, due to many factors involved we named the foundation, "The 13 Foundation" for all of our surviving children, and it is created to assist family oriented organizations and missions."

17

Bella's Smile

LISA AND DAVID were living the perfect little life. Both were college educated, employed with excellent careers, owned their own home in an upscale neighborhood, and living "The All American Dream" with one exception… they were unable to conceive the children they so desperately wanted to complete that dream. After many attempts, Lisa and David are now pregnant thanks to medical science, and now they were complete just waiting on their new addition to their perfect little family. Lisa's pregnancy was a good and solid pregnancy, and then they found out that they are having a double blessing, twins, and with the birth of the twins, their family would be complete and perfect!

Lisa's picture perfect pregnancy was a complete success, she was able to carry the twins to 37 weeks, and the babies weighed 6 pounds each. And if you ever met Lisa, you would wonder how she was able to carry 12 pounds of babies, in her small, 5 foot frame, but she did, and the twins were absolutely beautiful, Dax(Twin A) and Bella(Twin B). They went home to with their two beautiful children now in tow, and looking forward to and making all the plans that parents make for their children. Until one day when the twins were 6 months old, suddenly things began to change. Suddenly, Bella began throwing up at random times, without notice or reason. Naturally, Lisa and David took Bella immediately to the Doctor to investigate what the issue was, however no problems were found. Over the course of the next 3 months, and multiple visits and hospital stays, finally word came, and NOT one that any parent wants to hear about their child. Bella was diagnosed with a Grade II Astrocytoma on her brain stem. The doctors were not sure if it was operable or not at first, but thanks to her doctors they were proactive in Bella's care, and had a plan. Two days after finding the tumor on Bella's brain stem, they were in surgery to remove the tumor.

Bella's recovery would be quite a long and daunting recovery, since Bella would have to remain in the hospital for a month after her surgery, and then another 6 weeks in a transitional care unit, learning how to resume normal functions such as being able to swallow again. Bella was doing great through all of this process, and was such a trooper. During some of the worst times of the recovery process, Bella would smile the biggest ear to ear grin, and bring her little fists up close to her face and this somehow let Lisa and David know that everything was going to be OK. Finally, Bella was able to come home just two days prior to hers and Dax's 1st birthday.

After 5 months of in-home care from the visiting nurses, and therapists, Bella was doing very well and had almost caught up to her brother Dax's size and weight. Lisa and David expected that the tracheotomy that Bella had since surgery 5 months prior would be removed after the holidays. During the H1N1 outbreak of 2009, Lisa and David fought hard to make sure that Bella had the vaccine against H1N1, just to avoid any further complications that this disease had on the patients with weaken immune systems. Lisa said that they had done everything they knew to do in order to keep Bella away from anyone that might have been ill, and never left their home except for doctor's visits through this process, but somehow Bella contracted the disease anyway.

Within hours of the first symptoms of H1N1, Bella developed pneumonia, and then within the next 5 hours, Bella's lungs totally shut down. The doctors placed Bella on an ECMO machine, which pumps the blood and breathes for the patient, and Bella seemed to be improving. However, the doctors warned Lisa and David, the possibility existed that the resection of Bella's brain stem might not be able to withstand the trauma of the ECMO machine, and if complications from that arose that, there would be nothing more that could be done for her. On the fifth day of Bella being on the ECMO machine, Bella started to hemorrhage and late that evening Lisa and David held and kissed their little Bella good bye for the final time at the age of 16 months.

Through this event in Lisa and David's life, they have learned a wealth of information. One of the first things that they would soon learn is that parents of critically ill children have no other important job than to help their children through this process. Even at the expense of losing their jobs, their homes, etc.... Through the process of Bella's tumor and subsequent illness, Lisa lost her good paying job, and they became a single income family. Granted this single income family, was stilled considered to be middle income, they soon found out that there was NO assistance for middle-income families because they made $500.00 to much to receive any assistance from any organizations out there.

The second thing that Lisa learned though Bella's life is that what the Doctors Standard of Care is may not apply to every patient in every situation, and that Doctors don't know your child as you do. Lisa said "that if you feel that your child could benefit from something that isn't being done in their treatment, by all means speak up, you are part of the team, and don't allow the doctors to tell you otherwise. As the parent, you know your child better than any of them or their Standard of Care procedures."

The third thing that Lisa has learned is that regardless of the plans that you have made for your life, something will come along and change those plans, and change you forever. Bella's life has caused her to reexamine her life, and now has become a person that is much more in tune with other families fighting for their children's lives. Prior to this experience, Lisa was more concerned with living the perfect "American Dream Life" instead of being focused on the needs of others in the world.

Since Bella's home going to heaven on November 17, 2009, Lisa has been determined that Bella's short life would somehow make others life better. She wants Bella to become a beacon of hope for others as she has been for Lisa and David's life even through the tragic events of Bella's short 16 months. They started Bella's Blessing Foundation that assists middle-income families by providing a house payment here or gas money there, or anything just to let the family of another child that is critically ill know that they are not alone in the process. They don't fully support any one family, they hold up the arms of many, through Bella's Blessing.

18

Jeanie's Journey

JEANIE'S DREAM WAS always to go to the nations and share the love of Christ. This was something she had carried in her heart throughout her growing years and on into her adulthood. Every time something monumental happened in her life she thought, *"this is my jumping off point"*. She would wonder how God was going to pull it all off. Over the years, she had opportunities to travel with various ministries to different countries but nothing ever panned out. She just continued to hold the dream in her heart and then November 8, 2008 happened and the world as she knew it came crashing down.

Over the summer she had gotten rid of everything she owned and moved from Louisiana to Chicago. She just felt like God was going to do something. Just after her moved to Chicago she was given an opportunity to go with a group to Africa. She had a host family to help her save expenses and she obtained three part time jobs to start saving toward her big trip. They were scheduled to leave January 2009.

On Saturday, November 8, 2008 while she was at work, her daughter called. Her son, who was 24 and only had one semester of college left to complete his degree, had been involved in an accident and had been medi-flighted from the scene of the crash to the hospital in Shreveport. She said that she couldn't even describe the feelings that surround that type of phone call. She was dazed and nearly in shock as she went back to the house to try and get a flight out. She did not know it then, but the world as she knew it had ended. She spent over three weeks sitting in SICU waiting rooms, and when they finally left the hospital in February it was to be admitted to a nursing home. Her son had suffered a traumatic brain injury (TBI) among many other injuries. At this point, she says, "I did not know that I would soon be his sole caregiver."

It was over 18 months before she would be able get established with her own apartment so she could "bring him home." He also had to improve to a certain degree before she was able to handle him by herself. She said, "*I was so scared*. I felt very alone although I had friends and family step up to the plate to help me out here and there." But during this major life adjustment she lost herself. Honestly, she said, "identity had been something I struggled with even without this type of huge trauma and tragedy". As she tried to figure out how to deal with a victim of a TBI and mourn the loss of her son (although he was technically still here), Jeanie began to slip away. She felt God had failed her. After all, she had trusted Him to watch over her children, however, He had let this horrible tragedy happen. On top of the normal living grief associated with this type of tragedy, Jeanie had to deal with the loss of her own freedom, independence, and life.

As a general rule, Jeanie was a very social person. Jeanie is very outgoing and loved being in a crowd. Give her a crowd of people, and she'll know half of them by the time the event has ended! Jeanie was a people person, a schoolteacher, a minister…and now that was all gone. *She said "she was just gone;* and so was her faith. Life in what she not-so-jokingly call "the cave" didn't do me any favors as I became even more withdrawn and increasingly satisfied to be alone." Jeanie's independence was stripped from her and there was no way to fix it. Jeanie figured that one of two things must be true. Either God had changed His mind about the things He had put in her heart; or she had imagined them.

Jeanie spent a lot of time very angry with God for allowing all of this to happen. However, she found that she couldn't make it through the storm without Him. Jeanie had the Word engrained in her heart and soul and she really couldn't function without it. Sometimes that added to the frustration! Jeanie wanted to give up on God but couldn't. She found that she always kept running to Him with all the confusion, pain, grief and heartache. Nevertheless, her dream of going to the nations would just have to be on hold…or deleted. So, she concluded that God must not have meant what He said about her.

One thing that has been amazing to Jeanie through this process is how God has provided for this journey. She said, "I have never missed a meal. It's really been amazing to watch and be a part of. This really helped reaffirm His love and care for me." While her son was still in the hospital, early on she began to search online for work. She knew it was going to be a long journey and she would need to be able to work online. It took a long time but jobs slowing began to unfold. Presently, she has a solid freelance writing business and she tutors English online. Her first job teaching ESL was in the Philippines. She met with a group of teachers, and they talked about the school and then they had a Bible study. She was so excited she had to laugh and say, "Who'd have guessed"?

It wasn't long before she found another school located in Russia; and then one in China. She placed a map of the world up over her computer so she could get a feel for the part of the world her students were in. Then she started sticking pins in the various locations – just because she thought, it was cool. Much to her surprise, one day she looked up at her map at all the nations of the world she had been to through Skype. She had Bible studies in the Philippines, taught in an orphanage in Pakistan, prayed with pastors in India all through Skype. Another thing that she felt that she lost through this journey was her music. She used to be a "worship leader" for her church and also wrote songs. Her students in China – love to hear her sing. She always explains to them, "I only know church music. But they don't care, just as long as I play the guitar and sing."

As she looks at the map and sees all the nations, she has taught in, she simply has to smile. She said that, "All those pins that are stuck in the wall map in Brazil, Russia, China, Saudi Arabia, Egypt, Poland, Switzerland, and Germany are all reaffirmations to me that when God says something about you – or puts a dream in your heart – it's going to happen." It just might not look like you expected it to though. God hasn't forgotten about her or what He put inside her as a child. Again, she stated, "It certainly hasn't happened like I thought it was going to and I went through a stripping down in the process. However, what He says about me will always hold true. He is God and He knows right where I am."

#6 Points To Ponder

THROUGH THE LIVES of Misty and Bella, we have learn from their mothers in the previous stories that first and foremost, you don't have to take what the doctors are telling you as the only way to do things for your child. You have been given permission through these mother's testimonies to stand up for your child's rights, and if you believe that something should be done for your child's care, then by all means see to it that it gets done. Just because the doctors and nurses have the college education and the badges hanging from their coats doesn't mean that they know everything that is unique to your child and yours child's issues.

The other important facts that I would like to highlight about their stories is that in each one of these stories, there were angels that came through their lives and assisted the parents in some decisions that needed to be made. In Misty's story, Joann learned through a woman washing the floors that she should be in there holding and caring for her baby. In Bella's story, we learned that Lisa discovered that the Standard of Care procedures might not be the best for her daughter and that every child's case is uniquely different and may not fit into the Standard of Care model that the doctors and nurses were trained in.

You are the parent or guardian in your unique situations, and as such, you often times will know what are in the best interest of your loved one. Moreover, many times that still small voice will be telling you important facts regarding the care that your loved one needs. Nowhere in the bible is there any fact or statement that God has quit speaking to us or through us. We do find in the bible a lot of evidence that God spoke to Kings, prophets, and regular men and women with great frequency, and that has held true to even this day. God is still speaking to us today, so are you listening and hearing what the Spirit is saying?

Section VII

Golden God Nuggets Lessons Gleaned And Hope Restored

Ephesians 3:14–21

For this reason I bow my knees to the Father of our Lord Jesus Christ, from whom the whole family in heaven and earth is name, that He would grant you, according to the riches of His glory, to be strengthened with might through His Spirit in the inner man, that Christ may dwell in your hearts through faith; that you, being rooted and grounded in love, may be able to comprehend with all the saints what is the width and length and depth and height – to know the love of Christ which passes knowledge; that you may be filled with all the fullness of God.

Now to Him who is able to do exceedingly abundantly above all that we ask or think, according to the power that works in us, to Him be glory in the church by Christ Jesus to all generations, forever and ever. Amen.

19

Daughter Of Joy

I couldn't write this book without writing about my "Other Mother" Miss Joy. In order to understand this story I must begin at the beginning. One evening I had gone for what I thought was a Wednesday night church service for adults a this new church that the Lord directed me to a week or two prior. I arrive at the church in time for the 7 p.m. service according to what the secretary had told me and when I arrived there was only one car in the parking lot and all the lights are off in the building. This little car was a little strange sitting all by itself in the parking lot, simply because of the license plate. It read, "LUVED". Now as I sat there trying to figure out what to do next another car pulls into the parking lot, and out steps another woman, and explains to me, that everyone will be here in a few minutes, we all kind of run "Pentecostal Late" around here, but Pat is inside already.

This woman and I walk around the back of the building and the back door is unlocked, through which we can get into the building. As we walk down the dark hallway toward the sanctuary, I notice, that even the lights in the sanctuary, are not on either. We walk in and the woman turns on the lights, and there sits Pat, praying at the altar, with a circle of chairs already arranged at the front of the sanctuary. I immediately start telling the Lord, "This is supposed to be a church service, not some prayer meeting thing, you know how I am about these prayer meeting things, and how I am not into chasing demons on doorknobs." His response was short, not so sweet, and very to the point, "Sit down and learn!" I complied but really didn't understand why when I had called up to the church a few days earlier the secretary told me it was an adult church service and never mentioned that it was a prayer meeting. Regardless, here I was, and now the Lord has instructed that I sit down and learn.

At this time, the woman who had directed me into the sanctuary walked me over to the circle of chairs and we sat down. By this time, several other people had begun walking into the sanctuary as well and taken their seats in the circle. Once everyone including the Pastor had arrived, they all began to greet me, and tell me their names. The prayer meeting started, led by the Pastor of the church, and everything seemed ok, we weren't chasing demons on doorknobs, and that was a very good thing. The prayer meeting was over in about an hour, and we all went our separate ways. I thought to myself, well, at least now I know a few people that I can talk with on Sunday mornings now, and won't have to sit by myself next Sunday, and so on I drove home.

I have an excellent memory, almost photographic in that I can remember situations, people's names, where everyone was sitting, and if I think about it, can even remember what they were wearing at the time I am trying to remember. Sometimes, this gift gets me into trouble, other times it just drives people crazy that I can remember the things that I do, however suffice it to say, I have an excellent memory. Anyway, the next Sunday morning service comes around, and I am excited that I know a few people now and won't be sitting by myself during this service. I walk into the sanctuary about 10 minutes prior to the beginning of the service and there sits one of the ladies from the Wednesday night prayer meeting thing. I walk up to her, and as I am walking, I am running down the list of people and their names in my head, and for the life of me, I couldn't remember what this woman's name was. Therefore, I did what comes naturally to me; I asked the Lord, "Lord, what is this woman's name, I can't seem to remember it from the other night." His answer was swift, "Her name is Joy". Sweet, thank you Lord, and I walk up and greet her by her name, "Good morning Joy, how are you?" She looked at me with a very shocked look on her face, and says excitedly, "The Lord told you what my name was, huh?", I replied well yes, because for some reason I could remember everyone's name but yours and so I inquired of the Lord what your name was and He told me it was Joy. She smiled, hooted and hollered, "Thank You Jesus, Thank you Jesus" started weeping and crying, and it seemed to make her day. All the while, I am standing there, not understanding what has just happened, and here this woman has gone off the deep end of Praise.

She gains her composure, and begins telling me "I knew that the Lord had told you what my name was because that is what He calls me, my given name is Pat, but He calls me, His daughter of Joy. No one around here knows that, that is just what He calls me in our quite time alone, and it was confirmed to me one night at a different church meeting of prophetic ministers' years ago." Well, you could have knocked me over with a feather at this point, because at this point and time in my spiritual walk with the Lord, I had never had Him speak to me with a Word, or anything for anyone else, really I was quite new, to being able to talk to the Lord and Him answer back like talking with a friend right beside me, so this was something way cool for me at the time as well. We sat there that Sunday morning basking in the presence of the Lord, just enjoying His fellowship with us that morning.

Through the years of our friendship, we learned that she use to live in the same town that I was born and raised in and in fact her two kids and I went to the same high school together also. What a small world we live in, here we are some 60 miles from where I grew up, and I meet a woman that her two kids and I went to school together, her son and I were in the same grade as a matter of fact and because our graduating class was 710 of us, we didn't know each other at the time. As time goes on, I soon learned that her daughter was the girl that one day over the loud speaker in high school we were told that she had died in an accident on the Brazos River in Texas. Joy began telling me the story; the reason that the Lord calls her His daughter of Joy, is because she hasn't always been joyful throughout her life, and He was calling those things that be not as though they were, trying to make her understand that she was truly His daughter of Joy, and was full of His Joy, if she would only allow it to come forth. After that Sunday morning, I watched Miss Joy, seemingly blossom like a beautiful flower. She began allowing the Joy within her come forth, and was always a Joy to be around. After me speaking her name that day, it was as if somehow that one word set her free to truly be His daughter of Joy. She is now in the company, face to face with Jesus and she truly is a Daughter of JOY!

20

Rachel's Story

RACHEL'S STORY IS a perfect example of how all of our lives are connected, and how each of us can be healed and made whole through the process called LIFE. Her story wasn't included in the first edition of "A Life of Significance" because as most of us are, we are a little timid when it comes to admitting mistakes and tragedies in our life. What we fail to realize and God enlightens Rachel to the fact that through her pain she is to provide healing and comfort to the masses. Rachel is a highly talented writer in her own right, and she gave me her permission to publish her post from her blog as part of the closing chapters of my book. Not that this chapter couldn't have gone into any other sections, but I felt that what we learn through Rachel's Story seems to summarize the exact purpose of this book. All of our life stories contain healing for others if we would only share from our most personal pains, tragedies and triumphs!

This is a particularly tough post, particularly because it's so personal and I'm so private. My good friend who will remain nameless told me once that she believes that the Lord wants us to use what we've learned from everything we've been through to help someone else. It occurred to me as I was nodding off to sleep in the full-sized bed we left in Baby B's room that I can't bring light to anyone's darkness if I can't talk about the light that was brought to my own.

I really struggled with this idea because 1. I don't enjoy my privacy being invaded, 2. I hate talking about these subjects with people who I'm not entirely sure have my best interests at heart and 3. even though I say I don't care what other people think about me the truth is that I still do. I believe there is a fine line between being transparent to another's benefit and airing your dirty laundry for attention. Rest assured that I fully understand that the attention I expect to receive from the next few posts has the potential to fully humiliate me. I am trusting that they are a benefit to someone else will outweigh the risk of my temporary embarrassment.

So.... I was 25, newly divorced and head- over -heels in love with my then boyfriend. We'll call him Bryce, just to protect his privacy. My mom dropped me off at work at around 8, I clocked right in and suddenly felt nauseous. And HOT. I ran as quickly as I could to the powder room and lost the chocolate cake I had eaten for breakfast. As I stood shaking over the toilet bowl I remember thinking "That was weird! I didn't drink a drop last night, I haven't eaten anything unusual, I feel fine now that I threw up, maybe chocolate cake and coffee wasn't the best choice for breakfast." I went to work and when my backup arrived told her I wasn't feeling well and that I needed to clock out and go lay down in the break room for a minute. Her only words to me were "you are pregnant." I hadn't even told her I had been sick! I not-so-politely informed her that was NOT the case and that I didn't appreciate her saying that in front of other people.

A pregnancy test later that night revealed that I was expecting. I remember clearly the wave of dread promptly followed by another wave of nausea followed by another wave of anxiety that came over me. I talked my mother in to driving me to the store to get another pregnancy test because I was certain I had gotten a falsely positive result. Three more pregnancy tests followed by a visit to my doctor all confirmed my fears. I was broke, stuck in a dead-end job, living with my parents, unmarried and pregnant. And, I knew better. I had been raised....differently. I knew before I had my first sonogram or got my official due date from my doc when, where and how it happened.

I dreaded telling my Dad. I had planned on waiting until after I saw my doctor but he could tell I was upset. He came by work and picked me up to take me to lunch. He told me that he had no idea what was going on or why I wasn't myself but if I didn't want to talk about it we didn't have to. I was all grown up and it was none of his business unless I chose to make it so. I Blurted out the words "I'm pregnant" much more quickly and loudly than I intended to. I was embarrassed that I had caused a scene, scared that I had disappointed him and terrified that he was going to kick me out of his house. I expected the worst. Maybe because we were in public he would save the lengthy lecture for when we got home. I expected him to go in to shock and have a heart attack right in the middle of Schlotzsky's. He is really old, after all. I didn't expect the old man to laugh so hard that he almost choked on his bite of the cheesy smoky bacon on sourdough he was eating. Later that night at dinner he told Bryce and me that he chose to celebrate the life we were bringing in to the world and that even though we had made some dumb decisions he gave us his full blessing to get married if that is what we chose. He said he had always liked Bryce and that even though he wouldn't encourage one mistake to cover up another that we should think about what was best for the little one.

It hadn't up to this point dawned on me to think about marrying Bryce. I had just gotten out of a terrible marriage. I firmly believed that marriage was for suckers. I had told my dad (and meant it!) that I would NEVER be married again. I had told Bryce that even though I would consider leasing neighboring apartments that we would never be married. I really meant it. The next day we were driving to work and Bryce was talking about setting a date. I asked him what in the world made him thought we would get married? Over the next few weeks I mulled the decision over and finally decided that even though I loved him I didn't want to marry him. I also decided, however, that I would put on my big girl boots, suck it up, and do what was best for our child. I decided that he or she deserved family, normalcy and stability. I couldn't find a way to give him or her all those things and not marry his or her father. He surprised me by formally proposing at his college graduation. I tearfully accepted and actually found myself to be happy about being engaged. Already, this little baby I had unintentionally conceived was changing my life for the better.

We set a date. I changed my mind. We looked at venues. I rejected them all. We set another date. I changed my mind again. I never actually called off the engagement, but

I continually delayed the whole "wedding process". I finally confessed that I wanted to marry him but did not want a ceremony, reception, all the stuff girls get so excited about. I told him that not only could we not afford it, but we didn't have the time. I also finally confessed that to have another ceremony and a big white wedding would be to advertise that not only was I pregnant but that I was remarrying less than a year after my divorce. It was to be the scandal of the century. An advertisement to my previous failure. I didn't want people to think I was living with shame because of my pregnancy but at the same time I wasn't about to take out an advertisement. My friends and family had supported me once. They had shown up at my first wedding shower, bachelorette party, the ceremony. I didn't want the hoopla all over again. The last thing I wanted to do was this whole wedding thing all over again. My family conspired against me, and on January 26th Dad married us in front of a small crowd of our family and friends.

As I walked down the aisle at my second wedding I realized that I was excited to be married to Bryce. I felt a strange peace about what was going on. I didn't care that I couldn't zip up my borrowed dress, or that my hair was a mess (I had stubbornly done it myself) that my makeup was too heavy, and I remembering not giving a damn what anybody else was thinking. During the ceremony I cried so hard I almost couldn't get through my vows. When it was time for us to take communion, we had to fake it, as someone had forgotten the crackers! Then we started laughing so hard the photographer who was a good friend of mine scolded me for not being serious enough!

On our honeymoon, we were lying in bed watching the news and it started to dawn on me that Bryce was content.

I had been worried all along that he may have been in this to save face, or because he had to, or that maybe my dad had secretly threatened him with his life if he didn't marry me. I had felt totally responsible for throwing so much on his shoulders that I was terrified he secretly resented me for derailing all his plans. I was reading the paper and he was watching the news and I looked over at him and he smiled at me and told me that he had never been so happy in his life. It was totally unprompted, completely unexpected, and it hit me like a ton of bricks. I would never again doubt his motivation for making me his wife.

A few days after we returned from our honeymoon we went together for our 16 week doctor appointment. Just a routine exam. We went through the usual Q and A session, everything was fine, no concerns or complaints. When doc used the heartbeat monitor to try and listen to baby's heart, he had trouble finding it. He kept checking, and said that sometimes at 16 weeks it can be a little tricky to find. After several minutes of unsuccessfully trying to locate the baby's heartbeat, he called the sonographer for an unscheduled sonogram just to confirm that everything was fine.

The next few days are a little bit blurry. We left Doc's office feeling beaten up and shocked. There was quite clearly no heartbeat in our baby's chest cavity. I remember not really crying a lot, and not really buying in to the theory that the baby wasn't alive. We had been told that we needed to make a choice, if we wanted to have a D&C right away, wait and see if my body would expel the baby on it's own, or go to the hospital for an induction. We had an appointment a week later, and we had to make the call. Doc didn't recommend the D&C, as I would never have the chance to validate the life that had been growing inside me and he wanted to keep me from having a surgery if at all possible. I didn't want to go into labor at home, as he told me that I would need to bring the fetus to the hospital after I passed it. I couldn't imagine taking my baby in a bag to be examined. I didn't want to go to the hospital, as I felt like I should be able to deal with this privately and quietly.

February 14th was our next appointment. I had to make the call. I had yet to really open up about this, I was sort of dealing with a little denial. We had another sonogram to confirm that the baby was no longer alive. Bryce decided that the best thing to do was to go to the hospital for an induction if my body didn't start the process naturally. Doc set the appointment for one week later. We went to have some blood work done and to pre-register at the hospital, and I passed a good friend of mine leaving the hospital with her brand-new baby girl. She asked what we were doing there, as I had yet to make it public news that we had lost our baby. I knew she was already fearful about labor and delivery, and I didn't want my misfortune to take away from her joy. I blurted something about the baby's heart not beating and quickly walked away. That night we attended a Valentine's banquet at our church. We were congratulated by well-wishers and asked when we would know the sex of the baby. We awkwardly dodged the questions as honestly as we could without revealing the fact that the baby had died.

A week later I checked in to the hospital to be induced, so I could give birth to my baby that had been in my tummy for two weeks after his heart stopped beating. I had been told by Doc that even though it would be more difficult up front, I needed to hold the baby, give him a name and validate the life I created. I refused. I told Bryce more than once that I wanted the nurses to take it away before I had the chance to see it. I thought that if I never saw the baby it would be easier to go on without grieving the loss. Once again my family conspired against me, and at around 10:00 p.m. I met my baby boy, Barrett Logan Taylor. He was handed to me wrapped in a tiny blue blanket. He was just under three ounces, if memory serves correctly. He fit in my cupped hands. He was perfect. He looked just like his Daddy. Something broke within me. The dam came tumbling down and a flood of grief and sorrow threatened to drown me. In front of my new husband, my parents, my doctor and several nurses I had never previously met, I wept uncontrollably. I was humiliated. Bryce cupped my face in his hands and cried with me. He looked me straight in the eyes and told me exactly what I needed to hear. Those words will remain between the two of us, but other than finally being convinced that it was ok to express and acknowledge the grief I felt, something else started to break.

I had experienced one wounding after another starting in late adolescence that taught me that the safety of my childhood nest did not exist anywhere outside my immediate family, and even there I was subject to pain. I learned that vulnerability was weakness. I was convinced that if anyone knew how I really thought or felt I would not be worthy of love, and in addition, that was territory that was too dangerous to tread. Don't talk about it, chin up, get over it and move on. No one cares, and it's not worth talking about. Don't bring it up, as long as no one is bleeding, there is no problem. Let's not get mired in the muck of emotional intimacy. You aren't worth the time and effort it would take so let's gloss over the issues and convince ourselves they don't matter. Emotional pain doesn't hurt if you don't acknowledge it, so why go to the trouble to sort this out? Even if we did go to the trouble, that would require vulnerability and that's too risky, I've opened up and been shut down before. It's just not safe, and I'm clearly burdening you in my weakness, so I'll be a good girl and carry this on my own.

Laying in that hospital bed, unable to move or hide, I was forced into the most vulnerable situation I had ever experienced. My heart had been filleted open, tender and raw, and was exposed to this man I had known for just over a year. Bryce's refusal to allow me to carry my pain privately, his gentle leadership through rocky emotional terrain, and the tenderness with which he handled the pieces of my broken heart more than proved to me that I had become so hard-hearted that if I didn't learn to trust him I would squander a rare and precious gift.

God did not take my baby away from me. It was not his will for Barrett to die. He did, however, use my disappointment to work out some serious healing I desperately needed. Had I never been forced in to a position of complete vulnerability to this man that I have come to trust so completely, had I tried to carry this burden on my own, had I never been shown an honest appraisal of my heart, I may have cheated myself out of the incredible intimacy and close friendship I have with my incredible husband. It's been a process, but it started when he opened my eyes to see the condition I was in and how my husband stepped up to the plate irrespective of how big a challenge he had before him. I have always believed that God is always faithful to work everything out for my benefit. Even when it looks pretty bleak, he does what he promises us in his word he will do. Serving him does not mean that we will be able to avoid disappointment or pain, but it does mean that if we allow him to have his way in our lives, he will turn what was intended to cripple us into a source of strength.

> He trades beauty for ashes
> strength for fear
> gladness for mourning
> and peace for despair
> It is up to each one of us to decide
> what we will hold on to.

Rachel, her husband Bryce and their two beautiful children live in Paradise, Texas and she has her blog sight "just another day in Paradise" and can be found at: http://www.tayloredforthewise.com/

21

Gathering The Fragments

THROUGHOUT THE PAGES within this book, I have introduced you to some different issues of life and ways to see different issues that might be going on in your life. In this chapter I will gather the fragments and give you some scriptural basics of understanding to these different issues that some of us might have or observed throughout our lifetimes. Knowledge is wisdom when it comes with understanding.

We have learned that the conception of life is actually when life begins, not at another time during your pregnancy, but at the conception of that new life. We also learned that the desire for a particular gender in your much-desired child is sometimes a curse that has entered your life through traditions passed along to us through our family lines. Moreover, a final thing that we discovered is that your life, your life of significance is meant to bring

Glory and honor to our Father God and creator of your life. You learned that your life was actually ordained by God, and He already had you in His mind, and had plans made for you and your life. Every life is significant, and without your life, we all would miss out on what part your life is to interact with our life. We are all interconnected, and more interconnected that we realize. I have one such life experience where I learned at a very early age just how connected we really are, and this was well before the concept of six degrees of separation between all of our lives came in to the main stream of understanding.

I was a young 18 year old girl fresh out of high school, single and very pregnant, but I wasn't aware of it or should I say, basically had dismissed the thought several months prior. I was dating a little bit, but not anything really to say, but I had met a man that happened to live upstairs from me at the apartments that I lived at. This man was a sweet man, but not really my "type" that I would typically go for, this may sound funny, but just really too nice. With that being said, he asked me out one day, and I agreed to the date. Now, at this particular time in my life, I really didn't care about dating, and in looking back, I really didn't care about people's feelings either. However, I agreed to the date, and several days had to go by before we would eventually go out, and in the mode that I was in at the time I held the belief that I would just cancel at the last minute not caring about his feelings in the matter.

Saturday evening finally arrived, and so did my White KNIGHT. He arrived at my door, a few minutes early like the gentleman that he was, and when I opened the door, here this man stood dressed to the nines in a full white suit, and unknown to me he had borrowed a car from a friend of his to take me out that night. I stood there dressed in cut-offs and a tube top, and not at all prepared to go out on a date, and so began my tale of woe. See, I lied to him that I had just received a phone call that my grandmother was critically ill, and I had to go with my parents to East Texas to see her that night, because her time was short. Being the gentleman that he was, although I know that he was disappointed, he completely understood, and inquired if there was anything that he could do to help. I told him no, and told him that I really didn't have time to talk, I needed to get going. I left my apartment for the weekend to live up to the lie, and spent the weekend with some friends of mine so that he wouldn't see me around that weekend. I arrived back at my apartment on Sunday afternoon, and acted as if nothing was wrong and went about my normal routine. I received a knock on my door that evening and it was my Knight in Shining Armor standing at the door, wanting to discuss my weekend, and little to my knowledge share some of his own news with me about his weekend.

He came in and sat down as he always had, and listened to my tale of woe about how ill my grandmother was when suddenly he said; but when I spent the weekend with your cousin this weekend he said that your grandmother had died back in February, and this is now July, what's up with your story?" My heart sank, as I couldn't believe that this man knew anything about my family. He began sharing with me that since I had stood him up on Saturday night, he decided to go see some friends of his that lived in Tyler, Texas, and try to get over the fact that I had stood him up the way in which I had. He also told me that my cousin was the one that lent him the car to take me out that night since the only form of transportation that he had was a motorcycle at the time. He told me that as he was telling my cousin the story on how I had stood him up they soon determined that I was in fact his cousin that had done this horrible thing to him. My cousin proceeded to inform him all about the family relationship, and informed him that my grandmother had died several months prior to the plans that he and I had made so the facts were clear, I stood him up face to face that night, and lied directly to his face as well.

Things were never the same between us, and really I believe at this point in my life he was an Angel sent from Heaven, because, I don't remember his name I really don't know where he came from or even where he went. I have never seen my cousin since my grandmother's death, so I could never confirm the story with him either. Just one day he was gone, and nobody in the apartments ever knew him. The manager said that apartment was vacant above me and had been for several months, and through this experience I learned at the young age of 18 just how small of a world we really live in that angels are really among us. The other thing is that it is much better just to speak your mind and live honest and forthrightly then to try to lie your way out of a situation that you have gotten yourself in. The reason that I refer to this man as my Knight in Shining armor, even after all these years; is I truly believe that had I gone out with this man that night, he would have been just that, My White KNIGHT, white suit and all, and maybe I wouldn't have had to learn the lessons by the school of hard knocks like I have through the years. I don't know, but I have always wondered what would have happened had I been a better person back then, but such is the reason that God allows us forgiveness. Forgiveness to extend to others but more importantly, forgiveness extended to ourselves, because we are all learning and growing every day. And know this regardless of how many people you must forgive throughout your life time. The hardest person to forgive is yourself. My advice to you is that you should live everyday knowing that this could be your last. The bible in Hebrews tells us "Do not forget to entertain strangers, for by so doing some have unwittingly entertained angels", and you need to live it being the best person you can be and learn the lessons that life and death has to teach through your own life experiences and through the life experiences of others, and so was the purpose for writing this book.

Final Points To Ponder

Throughout ministry training, we learn and are taught to run our ministries with the principle rule of 80-20, which is that 20 percent of the people will do 80 percent of the work in your organization. They go further on to explain that in ministry you are to concentrate 80 percent of your time on the 20 percent that are doing the most for the advancement of the Kingdom of God within your organization. The reason they teach this principle like this is so that you can keep volunteers interested and motivated to continue their work. This is where they got me more than a little hot and bothered by their instructions, and I want to expound on the rule of 80-20 in terms of what Jesus did and how it applies to the stories within this book.

Jesus himself told us in Matthew 9:12–13 – "Those who are well have no need of a physician, but those who are sick. But go and learn what this means: 'I desire mercy and not sacrifice.' For I did not come to call the righteous but the sinners to repentance." Notice what Jesus is saying, He came to help the sinners find repentance not the righteous! What a novel concept, and one that we should take to heart if we are going to be effective in ministry. We should do as Jesus did, and concentrate 80 percent of our time showing Mercy and Grace to those without Jesus in their life, and only spend 20 percent of our time should be spent hanging with only our Christian friends and volunteers who are already well, and already have Jesus in their life. If we would learn what Jesus told us to learn in the bible that he desires mercy not sacrifice, I truly believe that the gospel of Jesus would move faster and reach more people, and grasp more hearts than if we continue to hang with our Christian Club members, and continue on with our Pep Rallies that have become the norm in Christian circles. Those people in need of a savior most often will not come to us and our Pep Rallies we must go out and reach them in their world.

The other point that I would like to make is that living A Life of Significance is 20 percent of what has happened to you and 80 percent of how you react or response to the issues within your life. In each of the stories throughout this book, every life that had tragedy or mishaps in their life made their lives better, and set them on a course to help others. They responded in a positive way to their situations, and we are allowed to glean the lessons that they have learned through their experiences. I truly believe that this is what Jesus was talking about when he told us to learn the lesson that "He desires Mercy instead of Sacrifice". Each of these people learned that we must show mercy to those in need, and not just offer up our sacrifices in some daily or weekly ritual.

Please don't misunderstand me I believe that it is important to have fellowship with other Christians. We gain strength from one another, but we who are with Christ, should only require 20 percent immersion with our Christian friends and mentors not 80 percent. We should be spending 80 percent of our time showing mercy and compassion to those without Christ in their life, and that love and compassion will do much for showing the love of God to others and will expand the Kingdom of God faster than what we are currently doing. Moreover, as far as keeping volunteers motivated and interested in their work, it will not be accomplished by us expending 80 percent of our time and attention to them that will keep them motivated and interested. It's the Love of God that is within them that will carry them through the work, and those of us that are the righteous should spend 80 percent of our efforts on gathering the fragments of those that are sick and without Christ.

I pray that this book has brought you peace and stillness within your soul that you are a significant person living, A life of significance. I also ask the Father of all creation to give you the hope, help, and healing for any situation that you are currently going through right now, and I pray that you will allow His healing light to guide you into a brighter tomorrow.

In Jesus' mighty name, AMEN!

About The Author

AFTER HAVING A one-sided debate with the Lord, I have included this to let you know even more about me than what you have learned through reading this book. I became a born again Christian on September 18, 1988 one evening at a Pentecostal Church in Hurst, Texas. Prior to this moment in my life, I didn't know the Lord, or if there was a God. The way I saw it was that we were just left to our own devices in this life, to make the best of it. I was raised to believe that the bible was only a book that was applicable to those thousands of years ago that ran around with tents on their backs, and of no value for us in these days and times. Looking back over the course of my life, I learned that God always had people, and angels watching over me, and the only godly influence that I remember is an elderly couple, Mr. And Mrs. Walls who were my nannies during the first 12 years of my life. I truly believe that it was only an answer to their prayers over me that protected me from some very harmful events that I would walk through throughout my life prior to accepting the Lord into my life. Throughout the events in my life where I should have died, I believe that it was only by God's grace and Mr. and Mrs. Walls prayers that allowed me to live to the point in my life that I was ready to accept the Lord as my personal savior, and friend that sticks closer than a brother does. Here I must share with you the story of how I became born again that night during a church service.

My second husband at the time had been telling me about God and Jesus, and that we needed to find a local church. Not that he believed that God could or would help him, but that I needed to find out for myself what God was all about. He instructed me to find an old time Pentecostal church where I would get the best dose of God he thought, and would find out what God was like. I spoke with the pastor of the church earlier in the week and he told me to tell my husband that we are exactly what he said to look for and please come and visit a Sunday service sometime. We went to the Sunday evening service that week, because my husband had said that would be where I would get the best dose of understanding of what God was about. As we entered the sanctuary of the church that night, I felt something very warm come over me. It was nothing like anything that I had ever felt before. We found a seat about in the middle row of the sanctuary, and sat down. Neither one of us said a word as the opening worship music played and then the preacher who was a visiting evangelist that evening began his sermon. I don't remember what the sermon was on, but I do remember what happened at the end of his sermon.

After he had finished his sermon, the music began to play again, and he begins to talk over the music and tell all of us in the audience that if there was anyone here that would like to give their life to Jesus, when the singer beginning singing the first word of the song, please step forward, and come down front. All I remember is that I stood up, walked to the end of the row where we were sitting, and the next thing I know, is that I am lying on the floor half way under the front row of pews in the sanctuary and I am hearing my own words that I had spoken to a friend of mine back in High school being whispered into my right ear; "You told me that if I wanted you be believe in me that I would have to come down here and meet you face to face and tell you that I am God." That night I believed and gave my heart to Jesus and was baptized the following weekend. An interesting Golden God Nugget about me telling you this part of my story is that I am actually writing this on September 18, 2011, exactly as God had instructed me, and when He told me to include this in the book. Dates and times are always significant with God, and He will see to it that your birthday is celebrated, as any parent will.

Not that I believe that everyone has to have such a radical conversion to Christ, however I believe that I had to have one since beginning at age 18 through the age of 21, I was addicted to drugs, and at the age of 20 I nearly died of a drug overdose, that my parents believed was post-partum depression. The only person that knew what was happening was my first husband at the time, and I believe if he hadn't given the drugs to bring me down, I would have died that night. Not that I recommend that you should self-medicate a person who is overdosing, but I am highlighting that drug users and abusers will self-medicate themselves and others in order to avoid the authorities that have the power to take their children away, or even send them to jail for using drugs.

Because I was suffering greatly from a Spirit of Rejection in my life, I didn't understand why I would go from one relationship to another relationship, looking for love in all the wrong places as the old country song goes, and never finding the peace, happiness, and love that I so desperately needed. A Spirit of Rejection can enter any one's life through the harmful soul ties of our dysfunctional families, physical, sexual or emotion abuse, the lack of love and appreciation for who God has created us to be, and through the harmful relationships that we will choose because of our lack of love for ourselves and others. Since the time that I accepted Jesus into my heart in 1988, He has continued his work of renewing my life, one fragment at a time. Freedom is a gradual process, and not an instant happening. Much like the slaves of years gone by, it takes a while for us to really accept that we are truly free from the bondages that once held us captive.

Since that time, I started teaching a bible study in my home in 1989, through that Pentecostal Church, I worked for another church, an Interdenominational church as their Director of the Bus Ministry, Pastoral Care Minister, Children's Pastor and Director of the Deliverance Ministry from 2003 to 2007, I graduated from Calvary Cathedral Bible College in 2007, was called by God in 2008 to start my own ministry called Finally Free Ministries where we assist people who are coming out of a substance abuse or domestic violence situation. We provide this assistance with transitional housing, daycare assistance; jobs within our many businesses that have been started to support our ministry, life skills education and pastoral counseling.

Our long term goals are that we will build Mobile Home Park communities called Eddie's Acres across the United States beginning in Parker County Texas. We have estimated that it will cost approximately one million dollars to build each park to house 40 families or individuals enrolled in our programs with an on-site daycare facility that will provide quality childcare to those residents and will serve the community. The average yearly cost will be approximately one million per year to operate each facility, which will be funded through the multiple business ventures that Finally Free Ministries generate.

People wonder why I am so candid and open about my life. It is because of the love that My Father God has for me, that He has protected and redeemed me and the things in my life to make me the Righteousness of God through what Jesus Christ my Lord and savior has done for me. I must testify of the things that God has brought me through, so that you too can know that God is no respecter of persons, and will heal, redeem and make you the Righteousness of God in Christ just as He has done for me! I call my candidness me taking my medicine, so that the skeletons of my past life don't pile up in the closet of my mind and keep me hostage to them. God has set me Finally Free, and He will do the same for any of you.

Suggested Reading List Of Topics Presented Within This Book

The Bible says: Out of the Mouth of two or three let a thing be established, so I have included a list of books that I suggest that you read on any of the topics that we have discussed within this book.

Abortion

You're Not Alone: Healing Through God's Grace After Abortion/Faith Communications (January 1, 2005) By: Jennifer O'Neill ISBN-10: 0757301681 ISBN-13: 978-0757301681

Adoption

Reclaiming Adoption: Missional Living through the Rediscovery of Abba Father/Cruciform Press 2011 By: John Piper, Scotty Smith, Richard Phillips, Jason Kovacs

The Father and His Family/Kenyon's Gospel Publishing Society 1998 By E.W.Kenyon ISBN: 1-57770-004-X

Death Of A Child

Safe in the Arms of God: Words from Heaven About the Death of a Child/Thomas Nelson 2003 By: By: John MacArthur

Safe in the Arms of Jesus: God's Provision for the Death of a Child/Kregel Publications 2000 By: By: Robert P. Lightner

Soul Ties

Healing through deliverance /The Biblical Basis–Peter Horrobin–Sovereign World ISBN 1-85240-052-8

Healing through deliverance /The Practical Ministry–Peter Horrobin–Sovereign World ISBN 1-85420-039-0

Blessing or curse, you can choose /Word Books By:–Derek Prince ISNB 0-85009-349-X

Judgmental Attitudes

I'm Judgmental, You're Judgmental: Healing Our Condemning Attitudes/Paulist Press (July 1999) By: Terry D. Cooper ISBN-10: 0809138700 ISBN-13: 978-0809138708

Making Judgments Without Being Judgmental: Nurturing a Clear Mind and a Generous Heart/IVP Books (September 21, 2006)By: Terry D. Cooper ISBN-10: 0830833234 ISBN-13: 978-0830833238

Marriage And Relationships

For Men Only: a straightforward guide to the inner lives of women/Multnomah By: Shaunti and Jeff Feldhahn ISBN: 978-1-59352-572-2

For Women Only: what you need to know about the inner lives of men/Multnomah By: Shaunti Feldhahn ISBN: 978-1-59052-317-9

The Father and His Family/Kenyon's Gospel Publishing Society 1998 By E.W.Kenyon ISBN: 1-57770-004-X

Health And Healing

Your Healing Door By: Greg Mohr and Forward by Dr. Bob Nichols ISBN: 978-0-615-20202-0

Scriptures to Live By: 41 Categories of Scripture for your daily life By: Greg Mohr

The Leading Of God Or The Holy Spirit

How You Can Be Led by the Spirit of God/RHEMA Bible Church aka Kenneth Hagin Ministries, Inc 1986 By: Kenneth E. Hagin ISBN: 0-89276-513-5

When God Speaks/Wagner Publications 2003 By: Chuck D. Pierce and Rebecca Wagner Sytsema ISBN: 1-58502-026-5

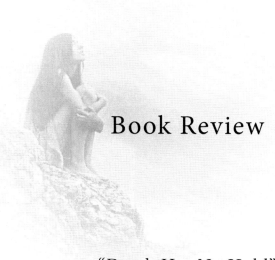

Book Review

"Death Has No Hold"
By Rebecca R. Brown

REBECCA R. BROWN and her NEWLY PUBLISHED book, "Death has no Hold" holds a special place in my heart. Not because she is our first author that we helped in a very small way with becoming a published author. Which is pretty exciting in itself, especially for our Editorial Staff members, Carolea and Nancy, but because she is a first class Christian woman with a heart to help others with her gift. Not to mention that I feel like a proud "grandma" of sorts. There is no better feeling than to know that you helped play a small part in someone fulfilling and achieving their God given dreams and calling.

Rebecca R. Brown's book, "Death has no Hold" may be a work of fiction, based upon a bedtime story that she created and told to her young daughter every evening. However, within each page you will see how she has allowed her God given talent of storytelling, to open up the Love Letter that our Heavenly Father gave for us to grow by. The characters in "Death has no Hold" come from the highest of highs to the lowest of low, demonstrating that God is truly the respector of NO ONE, and that time and space don't matter in the Family of God! The author takes you intimately into each of their lives to show a distinct contrast between Good and Evil in her character's lives and the consequences or benefits of each. The author truly captures the Heart of The Father toward all who know him already or soon will.

The most interesting thing that I noticed as I read through her book, "Death has no hold", was that through her characters you could plainly see people that you may know in your own life, and begin to have your spiritual eyes opened to the seemingly ordinary events going on around you. We are all connected, the "world" knows it to be six degrees of separation, and some may call it the butterfly effect however as a Christian we simply know it to be a Family Affair! This book is appropriate for all reading levels from 4th grade to adult, Christian or Non-Christian. I believe that we may very well see this coming soon to a theater near you, and if you are an avid reader you know that the book is always better!

Reading Rebecca's book opened me to receive a blessing that I had forgotten through a traumatic event in my life. When I wrote the first edition of "A Life of Significance" and spoke of my son that I gave up for adoption, I had always wondered why when I would type the name that I had for him would always be spelt differently and I had to "correct" the spelling every time. Then, when I found my son, come to find out one way he had spelt his name was the exact way that Rebecca, the author of "Death Has

No Hold". When I read that part in this "Death Has No Hold", the Lord quickened my Spirit and told me that was the actual spelling I had originally signed on the paperwork 33 years prior. Thank you Becky for being obedient, even in the spelling of names.

Congratulations, Rebecca, and many blessing to you from your sister,
Cammy Walters, Pastor of Finally Free Ministries and Author